needle felting

needle felting

20 cute projects to felt from wool

THE GUILD OF MASTER CRAFTSMAN PUBLICATIONS

Emma Herian

Contents

Introduction

Despite having been a creative person all my life, I only came to needle felting by accident. After exhibiting my hand-sewn recycled gifts at a National Trust fair, I was asked if I taught felting and if I could run a workshop. Surprisingly, felting had not yet entered my creative life, so I went off to research it.

Wet felting involves layers of wool fleece being rubbed and agitated with soapy water so that the fibres cling together and then being allowed to dry — a process that seemed messy and time-consuming to me. Coming from a background in three-dimensional craft (I have a BA Honours degree in 3D crafts), I wanted to push this further, creating new forms that needed a quicker and less messy process. That's when I discovered needle felting. This craft, with its simple techniques using a specialized barbed needle, enables you to mould and shape wool fibres into a variety of sculptural forms.

Since then, my work has taken me to teaching, selling internationally, writing and even appearing on television (on Kirstie Allsopp's *Handmade Christmas* on Channel 4 in the UK). I hope that sharing my creative process in this book will encourage you to start a new and exciting hobby.

It doesn't matter how experienced you are in crafts, or what level of creativity you hold, needle felting is forgiving for beginners, while its versatility and amenability offers endless possibilities for an enthusiast and experimental crafter.

This book covers 20 projects with step-by-step guides, hints and tips for you to make whimsical needle-felted creations. Relax into it, have a go and see where it takes you.

Emma Herian

Getting started

Tools and Materials

Needles

Felting needles are long, sharp, barbed implements with three or five sides, which are used to sculpt wool fleece. The needles were originally used on an industrial scale to make sheets of felt, but more recently have been adapted for the craft world. They come in a variety of gauges from fine (42-gauge) to coarse (32-gauge) to suit different types of wool. I used 38-gauge needles for the projects in this book. The sides of the needle have tiny barbs which catch the wool fibres, interlocking them together as you make a stabbing motion. The more you stab, the tighter the work becomes.

There are a variety of holders for needles that can hold either single or multiple needles, as well as a spring-loaded type with a guard that is perfect for children. The multi-needle tool is ideal for larger-scale felting, allowing for the process to be speeded up. Simply unscrew the top of the holder, place the needles in the holes and screw the top back on. It is down to individual choice whether you use a holder when making your projects. Some needle felters find them more comfortable and restful on the wrist.

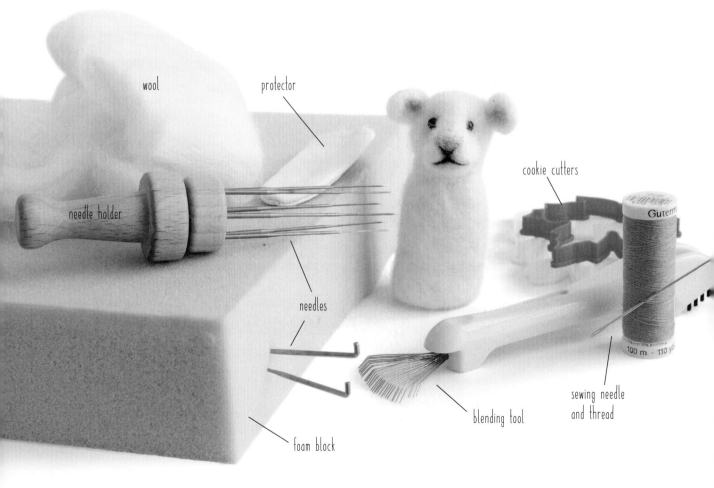

wool

protector

cookie cutters

needle holder

needles

blending tool

sewing needle and thread

foam block

While the needles are strong and can last for a long time, they may break if used incorrectly. It is also important to be very careful when handling them as you might stab your finger. Store your needles in a safe place when you're not working on a project, either in the side of the foam block, or in the small plastic tube that comes with the needle. Always dispose of broken or blunt needles safely.

Foam block

To protect the surfaces you are working on, it is essential to have a foam block to absorb the needle when it penetrates through the layers of wool. Use a firm, high-density foam at least 2in (5cm) thick and big enough to work comfortably on. You can buy these from craft or upholstery stores. When using the foam, try not to stab in one area all the time; use both sides and the edges, as this will prevent damage to the block or little bits of foam appearing in your work. Remove wool fibres from the foam block after each project by simply teasing them off with your fingers or using sticky tape.

Carders and blending tools

Carders act like metal combs that remove debris from the wool and comb the fibres in the same direction. They are also useful for blending different coloured wools together on bigger projects. The small claw-like blender is ideal to blend and mix coloured wool on smaller pieces as well as to prevent injury by holding the wool in situ when stabbing.

Protectors

Made from leather, these little pieces of fabric will offer you protection from the inevitable stabbing injuries you will receive from the very sharp needles. It is advisable to get them for the thumb and index finger.

Sewing needles and threads

You will use a variety of sewing and embroidery needles with threads for some of these projects.

This is a handy way to store your needles

Cookie cutters

These are brilliant for making a project simple; they are ideal for beginners and come in an array of shapes. I used them for the leaf garland (page 44).

Scissors

These are an essential part of any crafter's toolbox.

Hands

Your hands are probably your most valuable tools – not only for holding the needle but also for pushing, prodding and pinching the wool fibres into a shape you need. Don't underestimate their uses!

Miscellaneous tools

Other useful tools used in the book are a drill and drill bit, sewing machine and wire cutters.

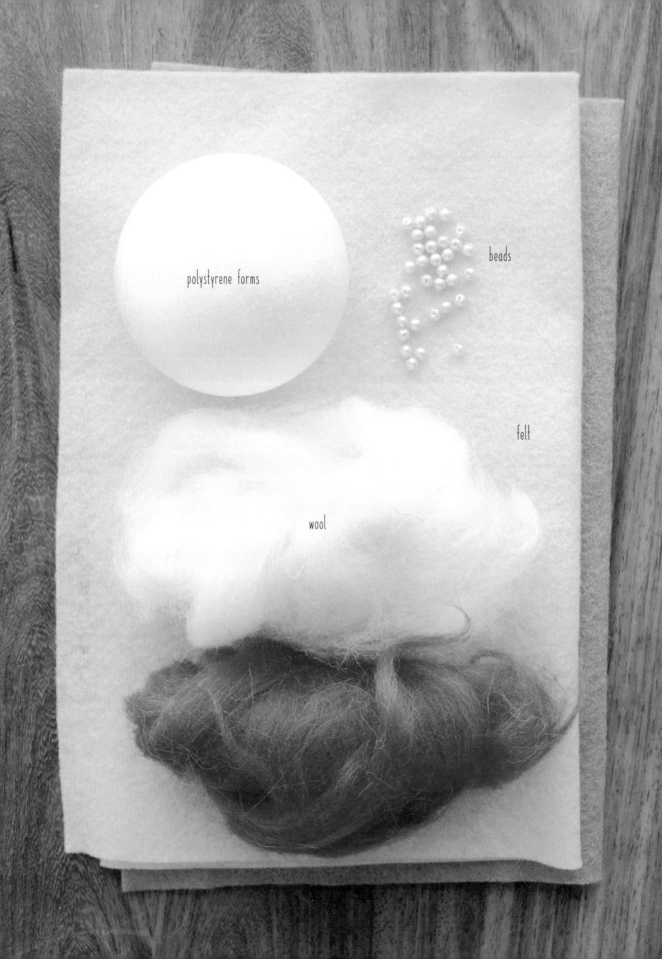

polystyrene forms

beads

felt

wool

Wool

There are various types of wool fleeces, usually named after the breed of sheep they come from, and some types are more suited than others to needle felting. For example, Merino can be too soft and fine, whereas New Zealand Corriedale has the perfect degree of coarseness for sculpting. Wool can be used in its raw state, but is usually sold having been cleaned and prepared for use.

There are two types of processes used to prepare the wool. Carding or roving is a procedure where the fibres don't necessarily lie in the same direction, allowing the fleece to be fluffier and coarser; this is ideal for needle felting. Combing is where the wool has been highly processed. All the fibres are aligned, making it fine, soft and slightly harder to use for needle felting, but it is perfect for wet felting.

Most of the wools can be dyed using either natural or commercial dyes. I tend to buy wool that has already been coloured. Having said that, I do use natural fleece too, especially Wensleydale or Blue Faced Leicester locks and curls, which are great for adding texture.

I use the words 'wisp' or 'wisps' a lot in this book. Wisps are your friend. By pulling a fine, loose piece of wool that appears transparent when you hold it up to the light and placing it on the piece you are working on, you can blend and cover a multitude of sins, giving your work a beautiful finish.

Store your wool in an airtight container away from moisture and moths, but allow the air to circulate every now and then.

Polystyrene forms

Some of the projects require polystyrene forms such as eggs, balls and wreath rings. Not only do they make a project easier to build, but also they will save you time and material. You will find an assortment of polystyrene forms in many craft stores and online.

Beads

Beads make perfect eyes for many of the animals in this book. They can also be used to embellish a piece; for example, the sprinkles on top of the cupcakes (page 72).

Felt

Ready-made felt is a perfect material to directly needle felt on to. It comes in some amazing bright colours and has many useful purposes. I used sheets of felt for the party bunting project (page 26).

Miscellaneous materials

I have used other materials in this book to finish or embellish a piece, such as wire for legs or stalks, ribbons and brooch backs. All these materials are available from any good arts or craft store or can be bought online.

Techniques

This section outlines the main techniques you will need to be familiar with to tackle the projects in this book. Once you've mastered these, there's a whole wealth of felting fun you can have!

Needling

Hold the felting needle as you would a pen or pencil, leaving the lower part free to poke into the wool. The needle needs to penetrate the surface you are working on but no further than ¼in (6mm) deep, as that is the only part of the needle that holds the barbs. The lifting and poking motion in a straight direction causes the fibres of the wool to mat together and interlock. The more you poke, the tighter the fibres become, giving structure to your piece.

Flat shapes

This technique can be used for features such as ears, petals and leaves. First, take a wisp of wool and, using both hands, pull it into a loop. Then, holding the wispy ends in one hand, lay the loop flat on the foam block. Using the single needle, stab the loop shape all over, working your way into the centre from the outside edge. Lift the loop off the foam and turn it over, then repeat the process until the piece has reduced in size, thickened in texture and resembles the desired shape.

POINTED TIPS To create the pointed tip on ears, petals or leaves, roll the felted end of the shape between the tips of your fingers, then stab it with the needle to hold it in place.

ONTO A SURFACE When needle felting a leaf or petal shape directly onto a surface, place the loop of wool on the area and stab the outer edge of the shape you require while pulling the wool to a point. Stab in the remaining wisps to the centre of the shape.

SPOTS For spots and dots, work directly onto the surface of the felted piece. For small spots, place a small wisp of wool where you want the spot, stab with the needle a few times in the same place, then wind the loose fibres around the needle and stab them back into the piece. If you want to create larger spots, use more wool and start in a similar way but stab a little further out around it when stabbing in the wisps.

LINES Felting lines uses a simple technique. Place a bit of wool on the surface you are working on, and with a needle stab the wool in the same spot a few times. Then, with the needle still stabbed in the spot, pull the wool with your other hand to create a line. Stab up and down that line to secure it to the main body of work, then tease off the excess fibres or stab them back up into the line.

Three-dimensional shapes

BALLOON A balloon or ball shape is a very useful structure. Take the wool and, with both hands, pull it into a fluffy balloon shape. Then, holding the wispy ends with one hand, place the balloon on the foam block and stab it all over with the needle. Rotate the balloon as you stab; the more you stab, the denser the balloon.

SAUSAGE Another useful shape for structure is the sausage shape, which is great for legs and arms. First, place layers of wool on the foam block. Shape these into either a square or a rectangle, then stab it all over with the needle. Gently tease the wool off the foam, turn it over and stab with the needle once more. Now roll the wool into a fairly tight sausage, stabbing with the needle to hold its shape. Alternating between stabbing and rolling the sausage between the palms of your hands will strengthen the piece and speed up the process.

Sewing on eyes

To sew eyes on any of the animals, first take a sewing needle and thread, tie a double knot at one end, and sew through one of the dents you have made and come out through the dent on the other side. Pull on the thread to make sure it is secure, then place one of the beads on the sewing needle and sew back through to the first dent. Following that, place a bead on the needle once more and carefully sew back through to the first bead. Then tie a knot around that bead, making sure it is tight and secure, and hide the thread within the back of the animal's head.

Beginners

Strawberry

Try this quick and easy tutorial to make a colourful and delicious-looking strawberry. Once you've learned the basic techniques, you could make a whole bowlful!

You will need

- Pure carded wool in red, yellow and spring green
- Single 38-gauge felting needle
- Multi-needle felting tool with six 38-gauge needles
- Felting foam block or thick upholstery foam

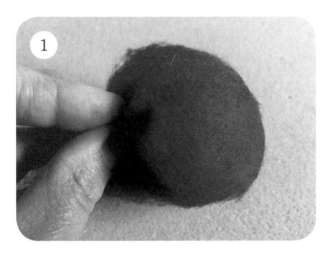
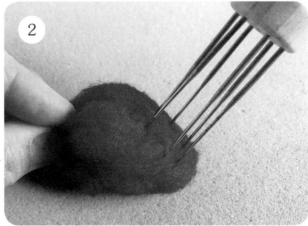

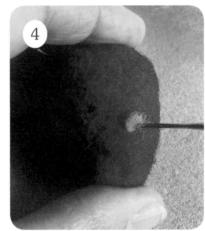
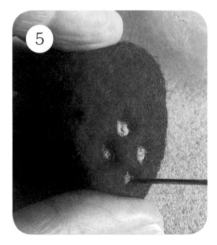

1

Pick a good handful of the red wool and place it on the foam block. With two hands, create a balloon shape. Then, holding the wispy ends with one hand, stab it all over with the single felting needle until the balloon shape becomes smaller and denser in texture.

2

Still holding the wispy ends, use the multi-needle tool to stab all over. Concentrate more on the opposite end to where you are holding, rotating as you go. This starts to mould the balloon into a strawberry shape. Add wisps of red wool if the piece shrinks too much, as this will help with the shape.

3

With the single needle, stab in the loose wispy ends to flatten the top of the strawberry. Add more wisps of red wool, rounding the edges as you stab to curve the top edge. You want to end up with a strawberry that is quite dense to the touch and about 1½in (4cm) high.

4

Once you are happy with the shape and density of the strawberry, add the seeds to the outside. Take a very small wisp of yellow wool, place it at the bottom of the strawberry, and stab a few times in the same spot. This will create a tiny dot. Any fine wispy pieces left over can be entwined around the needle a few times, then stabbed into position.

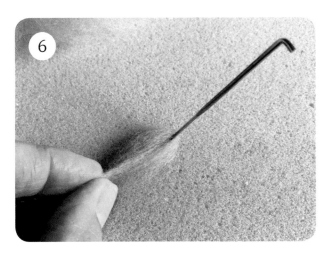

Make a selection of strawberries, each a slightly different shape. They can be small, pointed or with a flat bottom.

5
Repeat this step to create another seed next to the first seed, working your way around the strawberry until you have reached back to the first seed. Make another seed in the space above the two seeds and carry on in a similar way until you have reached the first seed on that line. Repeat these lines of seeds to make a pattern, working your way up to the top of the strawberry. Then put the strawberry aside.

6
Now make the strawberry leaves. Take a small amount of green wool and form a rough leaf shape by pulling the wool into a loop. Holding the wispy ends in one hand, place the leaf shape on the foam block. Using the single needle, stab from the outer edge, gradually working to the centre. Lift the leaf off the foam block, turn it over and repeat this process. The leaf will shrink in size and become denser.

7
To give the leaf a pointed tip, hold the top of the leaf at the rounded end, squeeze and roll between your fingers, then stab with the needle a few times to hold the shape. Leave the wispy ends fluffy.

8
Follow steps 6–7 to make a further seven leaf shapes so you have eight in total. They can be of varying sizes but no longer than 1in (2.5cm).

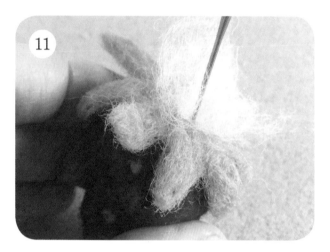

9

To attach the leaves to the top of the strawberry, take one leaf and place it so the wispy end touches the top. If there seems to be too much wool you can tease it or cut a bit off. Using the single needle, stab in the wispy end of the leaf to attach it to the strawberry. Repeat this process with the other leaves, allowing the wispy ends to cross over the top of the strawberry.

10

Once all of the leaves are attached, lift the leaves slightly and stab just under them with the needle. This will give the strawberry a three-dimensional look and help attach the leaves to the body of the strawberry.

11

Next, using yellow wool, stab a few wisps to the centre where the leaves meet to form a circle.

12

Finally, to make the stem that sits on top of the strawberry, take a small amount of green wool and form a rough rectangular shape measuring $1^1/_2$ x $^3/_4$in (4 x 2cm). Place it on the foam block. Using the single needle, stab it all over, then gently tease it off the foam and turn it over. Roll it tightly lengthways to form a small sausage shape, then stab it with the needle to hold its shape. Continue stabbing all over, leaving one end wispy so that the sausage compacts and forms a small dense stem. Roll it between your fingers to accentuate the stem shape. Then attach the stem to the top of the strawberry: place the wispy end in the middle of the yellow section made in step 11 and, using the single needle, stab the wispy bits into the strawberry, working around the base of the stem.

Party Bunting

Bunting makes the perfect decoration for any celebration, indoors or outdoors. You can adapt the patterns here to make needle-felted bunting in your favourite bright colours and designs.

You will need

- Felt fabric in orange, baby pink, red, yellow, green, turquoise, baby blue and cerise
- Carded wool in various bright colours
- 8ft (2.5m) of green bias binding
- Green sewing thread
- Paper or cardboard
- Pins

- Dissolvable fabric marker pen
- Scissors
- Pinking shears
- Ruler
- Single 38-gauge felting needle
- Felting foam block or thick upholstery foam
- Sewing machine

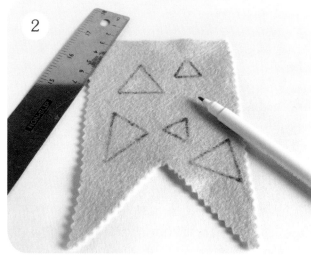

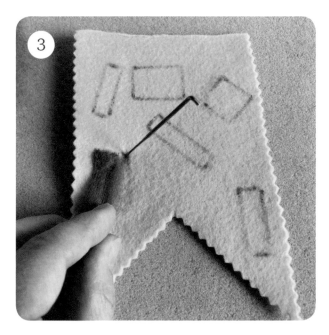

1

First make a template for the bunting by photocopying or tracing the template opposite onto paper or cardboard. Once you are happy with the template, cut it out. Now gather all your coloured felt fabrics. Choose the first one and pin the template to the fabric. Cut out the shape using pinking shears. Repeat the process for all the felt pieces so you have one in each colour: eight flags in total. Decide the order you would like the flags to go in when attached to the hanging line and put them aside.

2

Take one of the flags and, using a dissolvable fabric marker pen and the ruler, draw squares and rectangles in various sizes and at different angles at least 1¼in (3cm) from the top so that they fill most of the flag space. Repeat this process on the remaining flags but drawing different shapes such as triangles and circles.

3

Place one of the flags on the foam block. Take a small amount of contrasting coloured wool and place it within one of the drawn rectangles. Using the single needle, stab in the wool so that it starts to fill in the shape. An effective technique is to stab along the lines made with the fabric marker, then pulling the wool back to reveal a straight line. Occasionally lift the flag off so it does not stick to the foam block. Once the first rectangle has been filled with the wool, fill in the other shapes on the flag.

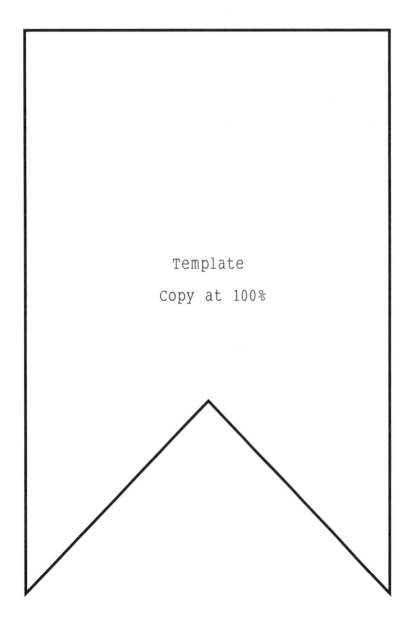

Template

Copy at 100%

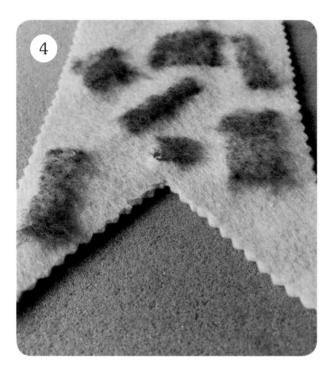

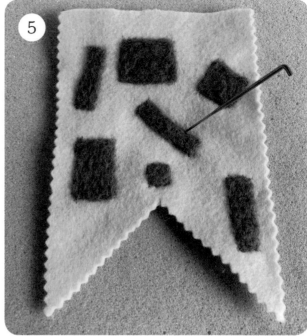

4

When you have needle-felted all the shapes, check the reverse of the flag by turning it over; if you can see most of the wool coming through, it has been secured to the flag correctly.

5

To create a crisp line to the edges, stab with the single needle all the way around the outside of the shapes, working any loose wool into the crease.

6

For the heart-shaped pattern, take a small wisp of your chosen wool and form a small petal shape by pulling the wool into a loop shape with your fingers. Holding the wispy ends in one hand, place the petal shape on the flag over the foam block. Using the single felting needle, stab the outer edge, working your way into the centre. Lift the flag off the foam block, then repeat the process with another petal

shape, placing it directly against the first shape so they start to form a heart. Stab with the needle to secure it in place, using any stray wool fibres to create the point at the base of the heart. Make a few hearts across the flag, varying in sizes. Lift the flag off the foam every now and then so it doesn't stick to the block.

7

To create the spotted flags, place one of the flags on the foam block. Choose a contrasting colour wool, place a small amount directly on to the flag, and, using the single needle, stab a couple of times to hold it in place. Then stab the needle in the shape of a small circle. Keep doing this and you will notice the wool naturally filling the inside of that circle. Gradually work your way in towards the centre of that circle while stabbing in any remaining wool. Repeat this process to make various spots in random sizes so they cover the flag. You should end up with eight flags embellished with various needle-felted patterns.

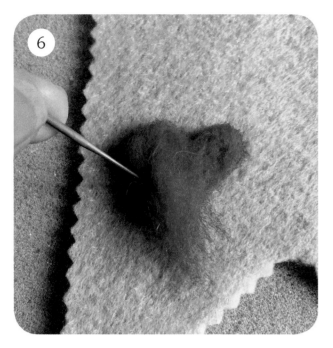

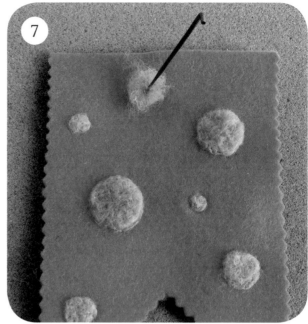

8

Put your flags in the desired order and put them to one side. Using a sewing machine and thread that matches the bias binding, fold the bias binding in half and sew a running stitch along its length for about 10in (25cm). Once you reach that point, stop the machine and carefully sandwich the last flag of the order in between the bias binding tape, then continue sewing along the length of the flag close to the edge. When you have reached the end of the flag, sew along a further 1¼in (3cm) of just the bias binding, stop the machine, then sandwich the second-to-last flag between the bias binding halves. Repeat this process so that all the flags are stitched safely between the bias binding tape with a 1¼in (3cm) gap between each flag. When you have reached that point, sew the bias binding a further 10in (25cm) as you did earlier and fasten off from the sewing machine. Tidy up any loose threads. Your bunting is now ready to hang up!

If you don't have a sewing machine, you can use strong glue to attach the bunting to the bias binding.

Toadstool

This red and white spotted toadstool is the type everyone imagines from fairy stories. Add the rabbit or the sleeping fox projects (see pages 110 and 122) to create an enchanting forest scene.

You will need

- Carded wool in green aqua, red, white, light green and dark green
- Single 38-gauge felting needle
- Multi-needle felting tool with six 38-gauge needles
- Felting foam block or thick upholstery foam

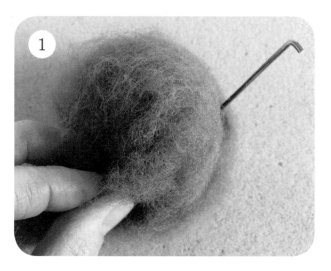

1

To create the dome base on which the toadstool will sit, take a large amount of green aqua wool and form it into a large balloon shape. Place it on the foam block. Holding the wispy ends with one hand, start stabbing all over with the single needle, rotating the shape as you go so that it starts to form a ball with a wispy end. Turn the ball over and stab in the wispy bits that will become the bottom of the base.

2

Turn the base back over. Using the multi-needle tool, stab all over to make the piece smaller and denser. Alternate between the single needle and the multi-needle tool to shape the ball into a rounded dome with a flat base. Add more green aqua wool as you shape the dome base so that it eventually measures roughly 2³⁄₄in (7cm) wide and 1¹⁄₄in (3cm) high. When you are happy with the base, put it aside.

3

Now move on to the cap of the toadstool. Take a large amount of red wool roughly 4³⁄₄in (12cm) long. As in step 1, form it into a balloon shape. Holding the wispy ends with one hand, place it on the foam block and start stabbing with the single needle while rotating it. Once you have created a rough ball shape, stab in the wispy ends, then stab all over to reduce the piece's size and make it denser.

4

To give the ball the characteristic toadstool cap shape, stab in some more wispy bits of red wool on top of the ball, to create a slightly domed shape.

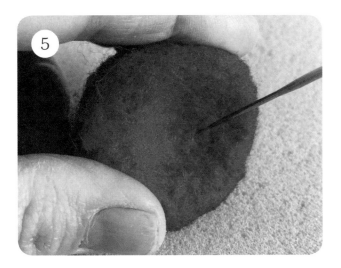

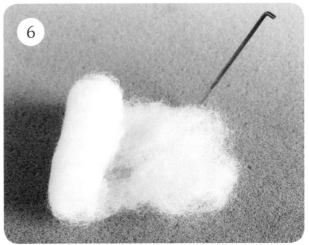

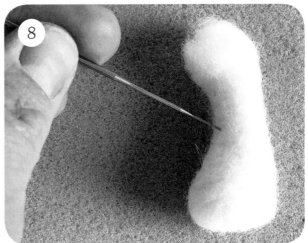

5

Turn the dome cap upside down and stab the single needle in the centre. Keep stabbing with the needle while working your way from the centre to the outer edges, creating a concave effect.

6

Next, make the stalk for the toadstool. Take a large amount of white wool roughly 4 x 2in (10 x 5cm) and place it on the foam block. Stab all over with the single needle, then gently tease it off the foam block, turn it over and stab once more. Roll the wool widthways to form a tight sausage shape. Stab it with the needle to secure its shape, leaving the ends wispy.

7

Continue stabbing the sausage shape so that it reduces in size and feels denser to the touch. Rolling the sausage between the palms of your hands will help to speed up this process. Stab one end with the needle to make the shape thinner. Then stab in the wisps of the thicker end to flatten it off; this will become the base of the stalk.

8

Add wisps of white wool to the lower part around the base to make it fuller. Stab with the needle a few times to one side of the stalk to give it a slight bend.

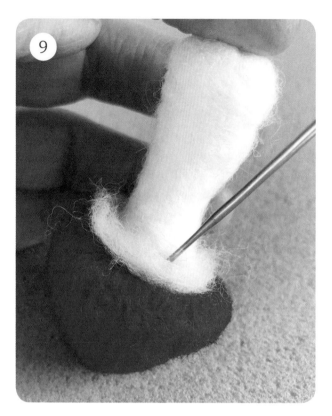

If you find the spots are tricky, you could sew on small white buttons or beads instead.

9

Once the stalk has been made, attach it to the toadstool cap. Place the cap upside down on the foam block, then tease out the wispy end of the stalk and position it so that it sits within the concave area. Using the single needle, stab in the wispy bits of the stalk; this will help adhere it to the toadstool cap.

10

Now add the white dots on top of the cap. Take a small amount of white wool, place it on the cap and stab it with the single needle in one position a few times until the wool forms a spot. Repeat the process to make a few more spots on the cap. Stab in any loose wispy bits that may remain; the more wool you use, the bigger the spot will be. Place the finished toadstool on top of the green base, take a small amount of white wool, and stab it in where the stalk meets the base to secure it into position.

11

For the final touches, take a very small amount of light green wool and the same amount in dark green. Pull them both into one small, long petal shape. Holding the wispy ends of the petal in one hand, place it on the foam block and stab it a few times with the single needle. Tease the petal off the foam block, turn it over and stab it again. Next, roll the needle-felted end between your fingertips to make it thinner and give it a pointed tip; it should resemble a thin blade of grass. Put this aside and make two more blades of grass.

12

Finally, attach the blades of grass where the stalk meets the base of the toadstool by stabbing the wispy ends into the green base. Stab with the needle a few more times up along the blades of grass so that they attach to the stalk as well.

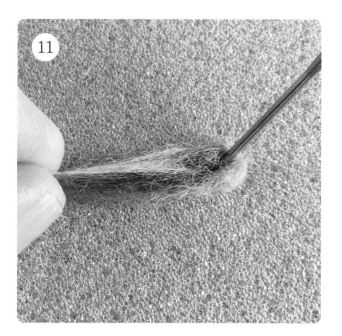

Make a few toadstools to sit on the base and add an animal in between to make a woodland scene.

Decorated Eggs

A basket full of needle-felted Easter eggs is just as cheerful as the traditional hand-painted eggs but much longer-lasting. Adapt the designs to use the colours and patterns you like best.

You will need

- Pure carded wool in lime green, daffodil yellow, orchid pink, candyfloss pink, white, spring green and baby blue
- Three polystyrene egg forms
- Multi-needle felting tool with six 38-gauge needles
- Single 38-gauge felting needle
- Felting foam block or thick upholstery foam

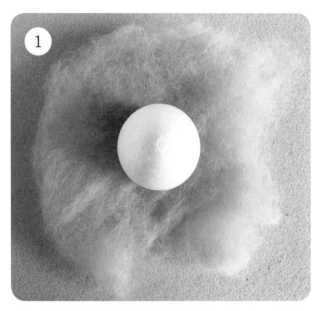

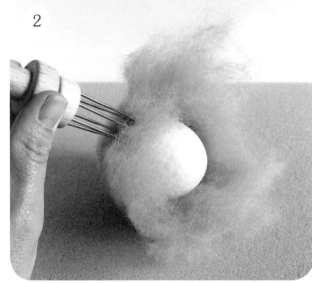

1

First, you need to cover the polystyrene egg form entirely with wool by directly needle felting onto it. To do this, pull a large amount of lime green wool from the roving, making sure it has no transparent areas, and shape it to resemble a square. Place the base of the polystyrene egg in the centre of the square.

2

Turn the egg and wool upside down and using the multi-needle tool, stab around the base of the egg to secure the wool in place.

3

Stab the remaining wool around the egg, adding wisps of wool to any areas that look a little bare so the whole of the egg is covered and looks slightly fluffy.

4

To make sure the egg is smooth and the wool has adhered to the polystyrene, go over once with the single needle. Then roll the egg between the palms of your hands and stab all over once more till smooth. Repeat steps 1–3 using the other two polystyrene egg forms using the daffodil yellow and orchid pink wool.

5

In the following steps you will decorate the eggs. For the yellow-covered egg, take a small amount of candyfloss pink wool and place it directly onto the egg. Using the single needle, stab a couple times to hold it in place. Then stab the needle in the shape of a small circle. Keep doing this and the wool will naturally fill the inside of that circle. Gradually work your way in towards the centre of that circle while stabbing in any remaining wool. Continue this technique until the egg has pink spots all over it.

If you struggle to get a sharp edge to a pattern, stab the shape first and then bring in the wisps.

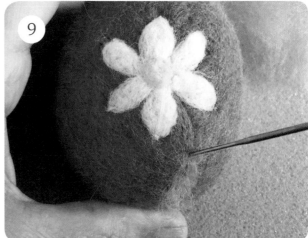

6

Next, take the pink-covered egg. Using white wool, roughly form a small petal shape by pulling the wool into a loop. Holding both ends in one hand, place the petal directly on to the egg. Using the single needle, stab around the outer edge to hold it in place, then stab the rest of the petal including the bit you were holding.

7

Repeat this process five more times to form a flower. You can make more or fewer petals as you like.

8

Now, using a small amount of yellow wool, place it in the centre of the flower. Use the same technique for the spots in step 5 and stab to secure.

9

To add a stem to the flower, take a small amount of spring green wool and tease it into a wisp. Stab one end between two lower petals, then continue stabbing with the needle in a line with a slight curve as you go. When you are happy with the length of the stem, stab in the remaining wisp of wool back up the stem and neaten off. Repeat the steps to create a flower on the other side of the egg, or add as many flowers as you wish.

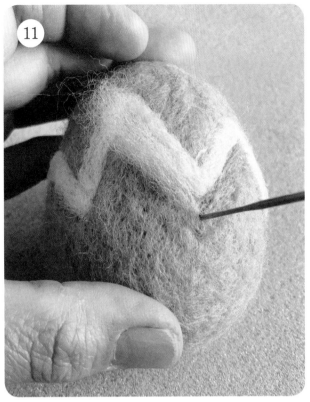

10

For the final lime green egg, we will add a zigzag pattern. Take a small amount of yellow wool and, using the technique for the flower stem, make a thick, short, straight line at an angle. Stab in any stray wispy bits as you go; if you stab in one spot and then pull with the hand holding the wool, this will help create a straight line. Stab with the needle to secure.

11

Once you have made the first line, repeat the process but starting from the bottom of that line and going in the opposite direction and angle: you want to end up with a sharp yellow V-shape. Continue creating a zigzag pattern all around the egg till the ends meet. If it helps, you can draw a zigzag pattern on the egg using a dissolvable fabric marker pen and then follow those lines. Now take some baby blue wool and stab a zigzag pattern just under the yellow pattern. Try to keep the points nice and sharp; if it doesn't look right, simply pull off the wool and try again.

12

Once you have finished the blue zigzag pattern, you can start on the candyfloss pink wool. Work the same way as the blue zigzag, this time following above the yellow zigzag pattern. Neaten off any wispy bits of wool. If you find that the patterns need more wool, use small wisps to fill in and create stronger, bolder lines. And there you have it: three decorated Easter eggs!

Leaf Garland

This project allows you to experiment with blending colours
and results in a beautiful hanging decoration.

You will need

- Carded wool in cranberry, orange, sunflower, emerald, spring green and light khaki
- Green embroidery thread
- Length of jute twine
- Single 38-gauge felting needle
- Felting foam block or thick upholstery foam
- Oak leaf and maple leaf cookie cutters
- Embroidery needle

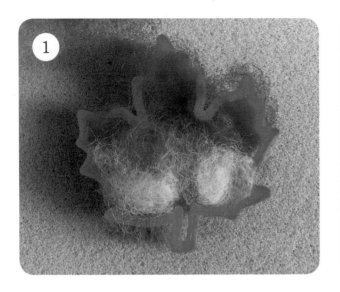

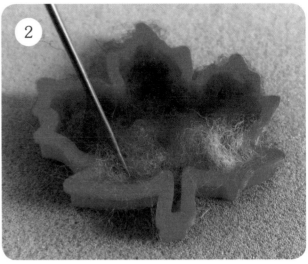

1

Place the maple leaf cookie cutter on the foam block. Take small amounts of cranberry, orange and sunflower wool from the rovings and place wisps inside the cookie cutter.

2

Push the wool down into the cookie cutter and start stabbing with the single needle, making sure you get into all the creases. Add more wisps in any gaps so you can build up a thick layer.

3

Once you have stabbed in all the leaf shape, remove the cookie cutter and carefully tease the felted leaf off the foam block. Check to see if there are any areas that have gaps.

4

Turn the cookie cutter and the felted leaf over, place them both back on the foam block with the leaf inside the cutter and stab with the needle once more. Add more wisps of wool to give the leaf some thickness while blending at the same time.

Be careful when stabbing inside the cookie cutter. You may find that the needle will break, so have some spares to hand.

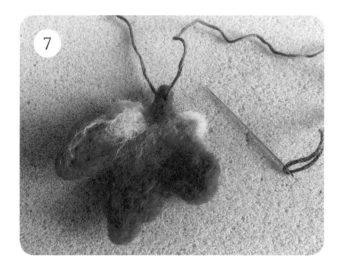

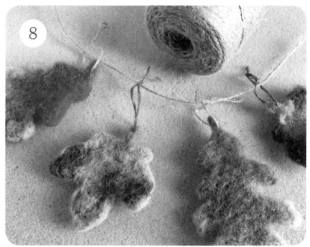

5

Gently lift the felted leaf and cookie cutter off the foam block and put the cutter aside. Very carefully, start stabbing the outer edges of the leaf with the single needle to add some definition. Pay particular attention to the stalk area; add some wisps of wool if it needs to be extended.

6

When you are happy with the shape and density of the maple leaf, create at least seven more using varying shades of orange and green, then put them aside. Use the same process using the oak leaf cookie cutter to make oak leaves in blended colours. Make at least seven oak leaves.

7

Once all the leaves have been made, take the green embroidery thread and needle and sew small loops at the stalk end of each leaf. Fasten off with a knot.

8

Finally, set all the leaves out in the order you would like them to be on the garland. Think about the colours of each leaf and alternate between maple and oak leaves. Thread each one onto a length of jute twine and hang the garland up.

Festive Baubles

Start a family tradition by needle felting handmade Christmas decorations that will be treasured for years. These baubles feature a snowy forest scene, but you could also make plain baubles and embellish them with beads and sequins.

You will need

- Carded wool in navy blue, white, forest green, green aqua, chestnut brown, black, red, bluebell blue and royal blue
- 3 x polystyrene balls 2³⁄₄in (7cm) in diameter
- Red embroidery thread
- 4in (10cm) of narrow red ribbon
- Single 38-gauge felting needle
- Multi-needle felting tool with six 38-gauge needles
- Felting foam block or thick upholstery foam block
- Embroidery needle

Try using different size polystyrene balls or different shapes. These are readily available in craft shops.

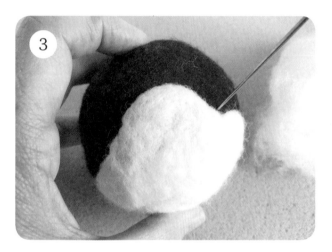

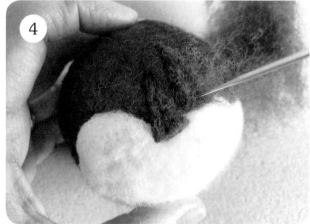

1

To make the sky in the scene, place a large amount of navy blue wool on the foam block, then place one of the polystyrene balls in the middle. Stab the wool into the polystyrene so that it loosely secures to the ball, stopping halfway up.

2

Using the multi-needle tool, stab all over the navy blue wool. Add more wisps of wool to fill any gaps. Roll the ball between the palms of your hands to smooth it. Then stab once more all over with the multi-needle tool so that the wool has a smooth texture and is adhered to the ball.

3

Place about the same amount of white wool at the base of the ball to make the snow in the scene. Using the same techniques as in steps 1–2, stab the wool into the polystyrene ball, stopping where it meets the navy blue wool. Take a wisp of white wool and shape it into a small hump. Place this on the ball so that it sits over the blue but blends into the white. Stab around the outside of the hump with the single needle to secure it, and add more wisps of white wool to fill it in. This will form the heaped effect of a snowdrift.

4

Repeat this all the way around the ball, varying the height and shape of the snowdrifts. Then take a small wisp of forest green wool and place it on one of the snowdrifts. Stabbing with the single needle, form a small triangular shape over the top of the green wool. Stab in any excess wool to fill in and form the shape of a fir tree. Create a few more trees using both the forest green and green aqua wool in small groups at random points along the snowdrifts.

Sew on some sequins and beads using glittery thread to give the baubles a magical glint.

5

To make the little cabin, take a wisp of chestnut brown wool and place it between two of the tree groupings. Using the single needle, stab over the brown wool to make a rectangular shape, then stab in the excess wool to fill the shape in. Add a small strip of black wool above the rectangle, stabbing in the wisps to form the shape of a roof. Use this technique to add a small square on top of the roof using chestnut brown wool for the chimney stack. Finally, create a little red oblong for the door, stabbing directly onto the ball, and two little black squares either side for the windows.

6

Needle-felt another little cabin using the same techniques as above so that you have one on either side of the bauble. Now to create the effect of falling snow, take a very small wisp of white wool and place it on the ball within the navy blue area. Stab a couple of times in the same place with the single

needle so that the wool secures onto the ball. Then wind the loose wisps of white wool around the single needle and stab them back into the same spot to create a small round dot. Repeat this technique to create various snowy dots all over the navy blue area, using slightly more wool as you get closer to the top of the bauble to create bigger dots.

7

To hang the bauble, thread 10in (25cm) of red embroidery thread onto an embroidery needle. Sew the needle through the top layer of the bauble, pull the thread through the wool and knot the two ends together to form a loop.

8

Finally, cut a length of red ribbon and tie it around the base of the loop. Tie the ribbon into a pretty bow and cut a V-shape at each end. Create two further baubles using different shades of blue.

Intermediate

Primrose Flower Brooch

Make this pretty primrose flower brooch to celebrate the arrival of spring. This would make a wonderful gift too.

You will need

- Pure carded wool in pink, yellow, white, spring green, leaf green and black
- Green sewing thread
- Brooch back
- Multi-needle felting tool with six 38-gauge needles
- Single 38-gauge felting needle
- Felting foam block or thick upholstery foam
- Sewing needle

Primroses come in all sorts of gorgeous colours so why not make a multicoloured posy of them?

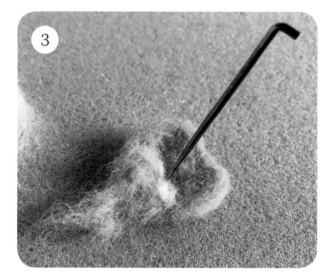

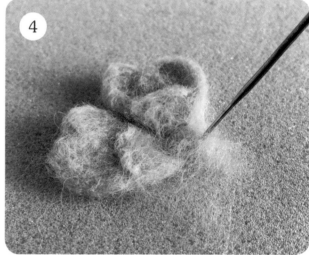

1

To make the flower, start by taking a small amount of pink wool and form a small petal shape by pulling the wool into a loop. Holding the wispy ends in one hand, place the petal on the foam block. Using the single needle, stab the outer edge, working your way into the centre. While still holding the wispy ends in one hand, gently tease the petal off the foam block, turn the petal over and repeat the stabbing process so that the shape shrinks and becomes denser.

2

Next, create the dent in the top of the petal by stabbing the needle a few times at that point. Turn the petal over and repeat the process until you are happy with the shape. When the first petal is complete, repeat steps 1–2 to make a further four petals.

3

Now decorate each of the five petals. First, take a small wisp of yellow wool and place it at the base of the petal. Stab gently, leaving a wispy end. Take a smaller amount of white wool and place it just above the yellow felted part of the petal and blend in.

4

Next you will need to join the petals together to form the flower. Take two of the decorated petals and place them side by side so the wispy ends cross over. Stab the wispy ends with the single needle to secure them in place.

Play around with colours and try blending in a contrasting shade when making the petals.

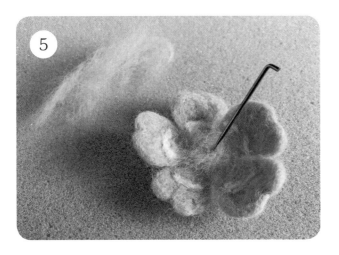

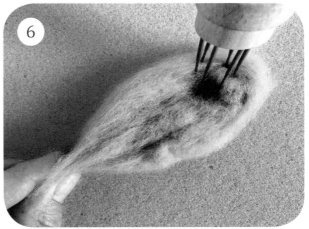

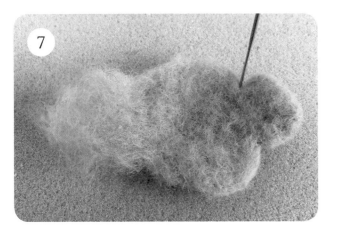

5

Repeat this process until all five petals are connected, using extra yellow wool if needed.

6

Once you have made the flower you will need to make the leaves for it to lay on. Take a big piece of spring green wool and form a rough leaf shape by pulling the wool into a loop. You will want this to be bigger than the final leaf size as it will shrink in the next steps. Holding the wispy ends of the loop in one hand, place the leaf on the foam block. Using the multi-needle tool, stab from the outer edge, gradually working your way to the centre. Then lift the leaf off the foam, turn it over and continue to stab with the needle. The leaf should end up thick and dense.

7

To finalize the shape of the leaf, stab with the single needle a few times along the side about $^3/_4$in (2cm) from the top to make a dent. Repeat this process on the adjacent side of the leaf. Repeat this step a further $^3/_4$in (2cm) from those dents to create the required leaf shape.

8

To make the veins on the leaf, take a small amount of leaf green wool. Using the single needle, stab a wisp of it at the top of the leaf in the same spot. Then, with the other hand, gently pull to create a line. Stab with the needle along the line to secure it in place. Repeat this if the line needs to be stronger in colour. To make the subsidiary veins coming off the main vein, repeat the technique but make the lines shorter.

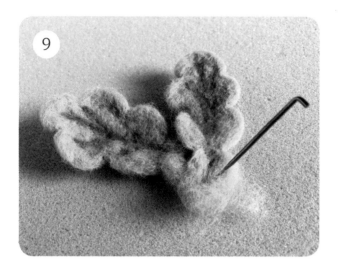

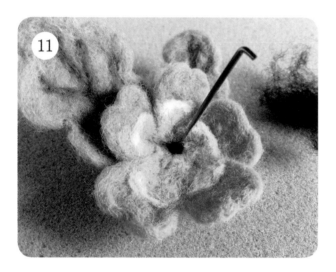

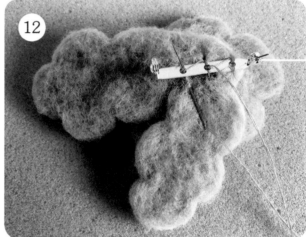

9

Repeat steps 6–8 to create a second leaf. To join the two leaves together, place them side by side so that the wispy ends cross over. Using the single needle, stab the wispy ends to secure them in place. Remember to lift the piece off the foam block, turn it over and stab the remaining wisps of wool on the reverse.

10

Next you will need to attach the flower to the leaves. Position the flower where you want it to sit. Using the technique in step 8, take wisps of spring green wool and stab in five lines. This will attach the flower to the leaves.

11

To make sure the flower is fully secured to the leaves, take a small amount of black wool, place it in the centre of the flower and stab a few times in the same spot. With the single needle, wind the remaining wisps protruding from the centre of the flower and stab them back in to form a spot.

12

Finally, turn the piece over to show the reverse. Lightly stab in any stray wool with the single needle and rub the piece between the palms of your hands to smooth it. The last stage is to attach the flower to the brooch back. Take some green thread and a sewing needle and sew the brooch back to the reverse of the piece using the holes provided. Fasten off the thread once secure.

Animal Finger Puppets

These lamb, piglet and chick finger puppets each have their own charm and character. Let them fire your imagination to put on a performance to rival any theatre production.

You will need

- Pure carded wool in candyfloss pink, sunflower yellow, orange, off-white, grey and black

- $^{1}/_{4}$in (6mm) black glass beads for eyes

- Black sewing thread

- Single 38-gauge felting needle

- Felting foam block or upholstery foam

- Sewing needle

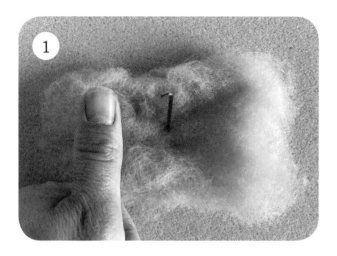

1

To make the body of the piglet finger puppet, take a thick strip of the pink wool roving that is about 4in (10cm) long and the height of the finger you want it to fit. Place it on the foam block and stab with the felting needle a few times, leaving the short edges fluffy. If there are any holes showing, place a few more wisps of the wool in those areas and stab with the needle. Gently tease the piece off the foam, turn over and then stab with the needle all over once again.

2

You will want a fairly crisp edge to the base of the body, so, with one hand, fold over one of the longer edges and stab a few times with the needle to secure. Tease the piece off the foam, turn over and stab all over again so that the piece felts densely on one edge, with the other three edges remaining wispy.

3

Now roll the piece of felted wool to form a tube so that the shorter wispy ends overlap each other and the neatened edge becomes the base. Carefully, without stabbing yourself, stab inside the tube with the needle to secure. You will find it easier to do this from either end of the tube to get right into the centre. Then lightly stab the outside of the tube to felt in any stray wisps. Put the tube aside for later.

4

To make the head of the piglet, take a small amount of the pink wool and make a balloon shape, holding the fluffy end with one hand. Stab all over, rotating as you go, leaving the bit you are holding as a loose fluffy end.

If you struggle needle felting the outside of the tube, cut a thin piece of foam to put inside, and remember to remove it every now and then.

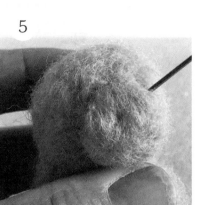

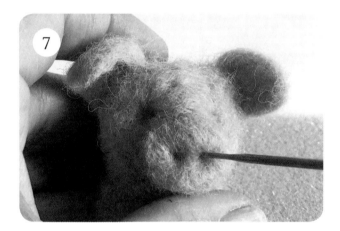

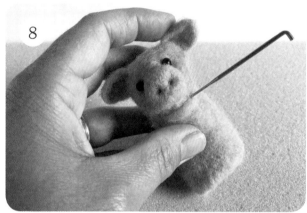

5

For the nose, make a smaller loose ball with an unworked end, similar to that above. Join it to the front of the head by stabbing the wispy ends of the small ball onto the head using the felting needle. Add wisps of pink wool to the sides to form a rounded nose.

6

For the ears, pull a small length of pink wool into a loop shape. Holding the ends in one hand, stab with the felting needle on one side to flatten, then turn over and repeat. As you stab away, the loop will shrink and become denser. To shape the end of the ear, rub the tip between your fingers and then stab the point to smooth the edges gradually, rounding towards the base of the ear and leaving a wispy end. Repeat this process to create the other ear. Once you have made two ears, attach them to the head by stabbing the loose ends to the side of the head, adding a few wisps of pink wool to either side at the base of the ears to secure.

7

To add detail to the face, stab a few time in the same place either side of the nose where the eyes will sit. Use the same technique to stab two dots for the nostrils on the front of the nose. For the eyes, with the needle and black sewing thread, sew two beads into position where you made the indentations earlier. Fasten off the loose thread and hide within the head.

8

Finally, to attach the head to the body made in steps 1–3, place the wispy end of the head into the fluffy end of the tube, then, with the felting needle, stab around the top of the tube to felt in those loose bits of wool. Then carefully stab with the needle up inside the tube to felt the wispy ends of the head to the inside of the tube. Then place the puppet on your finger and twist it round a few times; this will help felt the inside a little more.

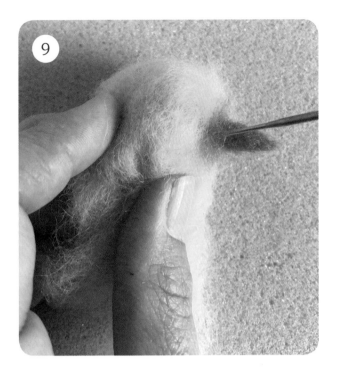

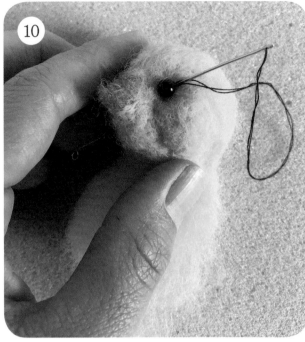

9

For the chick finger puppet, use yellow wool to create the tube body as in steps 1–3. For the head, follow step 4 using yellow wool but to make a beak instead of a nose make a very small ball in orange wool. Rub the felted end between your fingertips to create a point. Stab this with the needle a few times and roll between your fingertips again. Then attach the beak to the front of the head by stabbing in the unworked end.

10

Using yellow wool, add wisps just under the beak to fill out that area. Add larger pieces of wool either side of the beak to create the cheeks of the chick, adding more wisps to blend and cover any obvious lines. For the eyes, stab indentations either side of the beak and sew on beads as in step 7. Finally, follow the instructions in step 8 to attach the head to the tube.

11

To make the lamb finger puppet, use off-white wool and follow steps 1–3 to create the tube for the body, then follow steps 4–5 to make the head and the nose. To create the shape of the face, stab a few times in the same place either side of the nose to create indentations where the eyes will sit. Then stab a V-shaped line at the tip of the nose and a smaller upside-down V-line just under to form the mouth. For the ears, follow step 6 using off-white wool. Also blend in light wisps of pink to the inside of each ear before finally attaching them to the head.

12

For the final details of the face, add a very small amount of grey wool to the tip of the nose, blending it in with a bit of off-white, then a small amount of pink wool below the mouth. Take a small wisp of black wool and stab it into the lines of the nose and mouth you created when shaping the face in step 11. Using the needle and thread, sew on two black beads for the eyes. Fasten off the thread and hide the loose ends within the head. Finally, attach the lamb's head to the tube body as in step 8. Now your three puppets are ready to star in your own theatrical production!

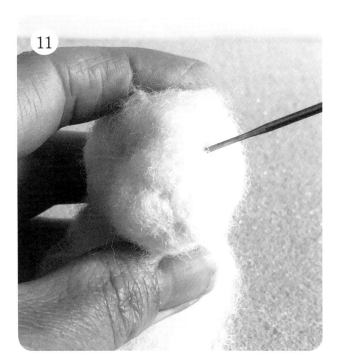

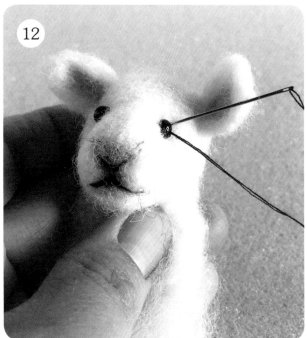

Daisy Sculpture

Make an ever-lasting touch of summer with this needle-felted daisy sculpture, which is displayed in its own branch container.

You will need

- Pure carded wool in white, spring green, daffodil yellow, sunflower yellow
- Length of beading wire
- Tree branch roughly 2¼in (6cm) in diameter
- Single 38-gauge felting needle
- Multi-needle felting tool with six 38-gauge needles
- Felting foam block or upholstery foam
- Glue gun and PVA glue
- Wire cutters
- Drill with 4.5mm bit

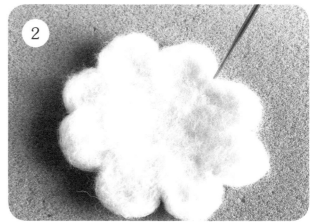

1

First, make the base layer of petals. Take some white wool and place it on the foam block. Shape it into a rough circle measuring about 3¼in (8cm) in diameter. If there are any gaps in the circle, place a few wisps of white wool over the top. Next, using the multi-needle tool, stab all over and around the edge a few times. Gently tease the circle off the foam block, turn it over and repeat the process so that the circle shrinks in size to about 2¾in (7cm) in diameter and is dense in texture.

2

To turn the circle into a flower shape, stab with the single needle in one spot at the edge of the circle a few times to make a dent. Repeat the same step opposite the first dent and then another in between those two dents, then opposite that one. You should end up with what looks like a flower shape with four petals. Next you will need to make further dents in between the four already made so that you end up with an eight-petalled flower. Put this shape aside for later.

3

Now make eight individual petals that will sit on top of the base layer. Take a wisp of white wool and form a rough petal shape by pulling the wool into a loop. Holding the wispy ends with one hand, place the shape on the foam block and stab all over with the single needle.

4

Lift the petal off the foam block, turn it over and repeat this process so that the petal becomes smaller in size and denser in texture. You can rub the petal between your fingers to speed up the felting process while leaving the wispy end unworked. Repeat this step to make a further seven petals.

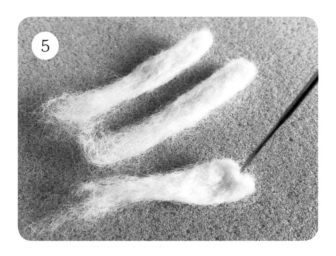

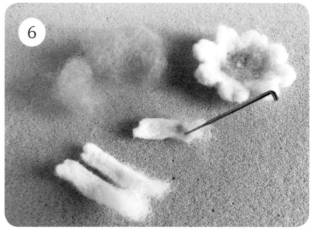

5

To shape the petal tips, use the technique from step 2 to make a dent in the rounded end. Follow this process for all of the petals.

6

Take a small wisp of spring green wool, place it towards the wispy end of the petal and stab in place to secure. Turn the petal over and stab once more. This will give a blended look to the petal. Do the same to the middle of the large flower made in steps 1–2.

7

Once all the petals have been made, attach them to the main flower. Take one of the petals and place it so it sits between two of the dents on the large flower with the wispy end sitting in the centre. Using the single needle, stab in the wispy bits so that it secures the petals to the large flower. Repeat this process, attaching the rest of the petals so they sit between each of the dents. If some of the wispy ends are too long, simply tease them off the petal before attaching. Turn the flower over and lightly stab in any wispy bits that have come through to the other side.

8

For the centre of the flower, place a small amount of daffodil yellow wool in the middle and stab with the needle to secure. To create a domed shape, add a little sunflower yellow wool in the middle on top and stab all over for a smooth finish.

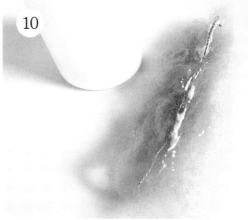

9

To create some texture, with the single needle, stab a few times in one place on the yellow dome to create an indentation, then do the same all over the dome to create the required texture. Put the flower aside.

10

To make a stem for the flower, cut 10in (25cm) of beading wire and fold it in half. Then, holding the folded end, twist the two lengths of wire together. Take a piece of spring green wool the length of the wire and twice the width. Lay the wool down flat on some clean paper and dab a small amount of PVA glue up the middle of its length. Place the twisted wire in the centre, twist the wool around it, carefully wipe off any glue residue and give it another twist. Place the stem on the foam block and, using the single needle, stab both of the wispy ends to stop the wool from unwinding. Put aside to allow it to dry.

11

Once dried, place one end of the stem to the back of the flower so it sits in the middle. Take a small piece of the green wool and place it over the top of the stem. With a single needle carefully stab around the stem and lightly over the top so that the stem is secured to the flower. Put the flower and stem to one side for later.

12

Finally, make a base to hold your flower. Cut the branch to the height you would like. Using the drill, make a hole in the centre of the branch at least 2in (5cm) deep. Add a dab of glue in the hole and push the stem inside. Wipe off any glue residue and put the flower aside to dry.

You can use any type of vessel to hold the daisy if you can't find a suitable tree branch.

Cupcakes

Enjoy making these playful cupcakes complete with colourful sprinkles. They look almost good enough to eat!

You will need

- Pure carded wool in white, beige, caramel, candyfloss pink, magenta and lilac
- Sewing thread in pink, white and lilac
- Selection of bugle and round pearl beads
- Multi-needle felting tool with six 38-gauge needles
- Single 38-gauge felting needle
- Felting foam block or thick upholstery foam
- Sewing needle

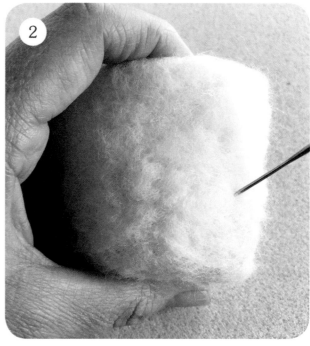

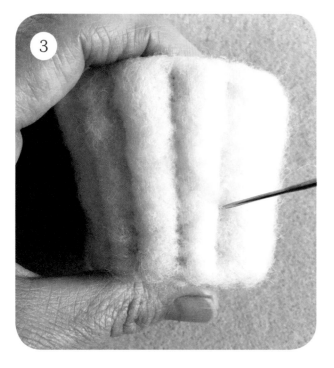

1

For the cupcake casing, take a large amount of white wool and shape it into rectangle measuring roughly 6¼ x 5½in (16 x 14cm). Lay a small amount of beige wool over the top. Place it on the foam block and stab all over using the multi-needle tool. Gently lift the rectangle off the foam block, turn it over and stab again all over once more.

2

Roll the rectangle widthways to form a short, fat sausage shape. Stab with the single needle to hold its shape, then stab at the base of the sausage to create a flat bottom to the cupcake case. Next, using the single needle, add some more white wool around the top half of the cup case, stabbing it in position while flattening the top. You should end up with a rough cupcake case shape, fatter at the top and narrower at the base while being dense and solid.

3

To create the ribbed effect around the outside edge of the casing, stab the single needle from the top to the base in a vertical line. Once you have reached the base, go over the line with the needle once more. Make another line about ³⁄₈in (1cm) away. Do this all the way around the casing until you reach the first line.

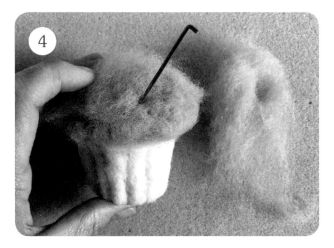

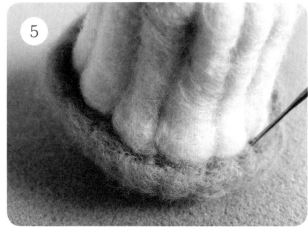

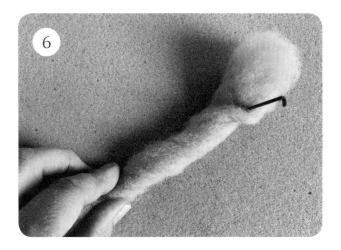

4

Once the base of the cupcake has been made, start adding some beige wool to the top to create a wide domed shape that will form the cake part. When you have achieved a rough dome shape, start stabbing in some of the caramel wool over the top. Keep stabbing with the single needle so that the dome becomes flatter in shape, allowing the cake to expand over the edge of the casing.

5

Turn the cupcake upside down and stab the underside of the cake; this will help tie the cake topping into the casing and round off the edge.

6

Now that the cake and casing have been made, it is time to add the icing on the top. Pull a long length of candyfloss pink wool from the roving and place it on the foam block. Twist lightly then stab all over a few times with the single needle.

7

Next place one of the wispy ends of the icing on the top of the cake towards the outer edge and stab with the single needle to secure in place. Then gradually lay it around the outer edge of the cake, stabbing lightly with the single needle to hold it in position until you meet the point where you started. Now start laying the icing over the inner edge of the first layer so that it starts to swirl up in height and make a spiral pattern, stabbing with the needle every now and then to hold in place. To accentuate the swirl of icing, stab with the needle in the creases while stabbing all over the icing lightly, working along the spiral to the top. This will adhere the icing to the cake as well as felting it into a dense texture.

8

Decorate the icing with a little needle-felted heart. Take a small amount of magenta wool and pull it into a loop. Hold the wispy ends with one hand and stab with the single needle all over. Lift it off the foam and turn it over, then stab once more so that it becomes a small petal shape.

9

Repeat this process to make another petal shape, then place the two side by side on the foam block with the wispy ends meeting at the bottom. Stab with the single needle to join the two petals together by placing a wisp of magenta wool over the join, incorporating any other wisps of wool. Remember to lift the heart off the foam block, turn over and stab again with the needle. You can shape the bottom point of the heart by gently squeezing the tip between your fingers, and tidy up any stray wisps by stabbing them back into the heart.

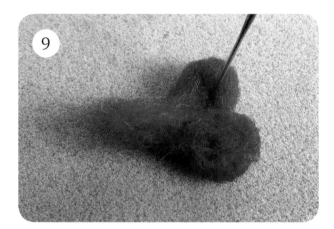

10

Place the heart on top of the icing swirl and stab with the needle at its base to secure it on top of the icing. Take a selection of bugle beads to make the sprinkles on top of the icing. Thread the needle with pink thread and make a double knot at one end. Sew the first bit of thread into the crease of the icing to hide the knot, then sew on each bugle bead, hiding the thread under the icing as you work from the top. Sew the beads on in random places, then fasten off the thread with the knot around the final bead and hide the thread within the icing. Repeat all the steps to create other cupcakes with white icing and lilac icing. Add some pearl beads for sprinkles along with the bugle beads.

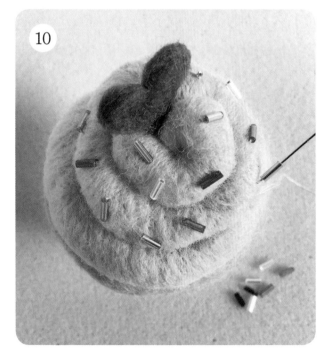

Play around with the type of icing. You can make it as ornate or as plain as you like.

These cupcakes would also make great pin cushions. Use some pretty pins as decoration.

Acorn Brooch

As needle-felted projects are often quite small in scale, they can easily be adapted into unique jewellery pieces. Here you can turn a little acorn and oak leaf into a pretty brooch.

You will need

- Carded wool in leaf green, lime green, chestnut brown and caramel
- Green sewing thread
- Brooch back
- Single 38-gauge felting needle
- Felting foam block or thick upholstery foam
- Sewing needle

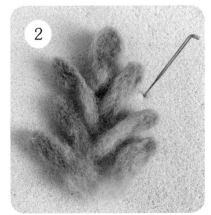

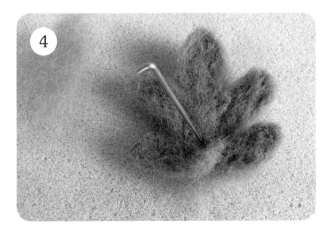

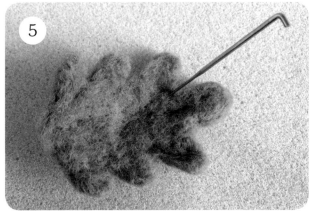

1

First, make the leaf from which the acorn will hang. Take a small amount of leaf green wool and form a rough petal shape by pulling the wool into a loop. Holding the wispy ends with one hand, place the petal on the foam block and stab it all over with the single needle, leaving the ends wispy. Lift the petal off the foam block and turn it over, stabbing with the needle once more. Put the petal shape aside.

2

Repeat this process to make six more rough petal shapes. Once you have made seven petal shapes, place them on the foam block to check that they will form a rough oak leaf shape, with the wispy ends overlapping each other.

3

To join the petals together and to form the oak leaf, take the top three petals and place them so the wispy ends overlap each other. Stab all over with the single needle to secure the shapes to each other. Occasionally turn the leaf over on the foam block, stabbing once more with the needle.

4

Once the first set of petal shapes are attached, take the next two and place them just below so that they overlap slightly. Again, using the single needle, stab in the wispy bits so they adhere to the first three shapes. Repeat these steps for the remaining two petal shapes, remembering to lift them off the foam block occasionally. You should end up with a rough oak leaf shape.

5

Next, using the single needle, stab all the way around the outer edge of the leaf, rounding and smoothing the pointed lobed parts and stabbing in any stray wisps of wool.

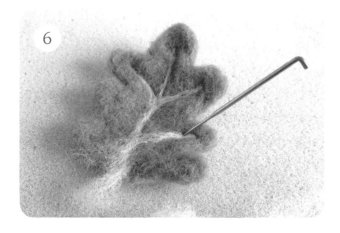

6

Now move on to the veins of the leaf. Take a small amount of lime green wool and place it at the top end of the leaf. Stab the wool a few times in the same spot, then, with the needle still in the leaf, pull the wool with your other hand to create a line down the centre of the leaf. Stab up and down along that line with the needle to secure it in position. Remember to lift the whole piece off the foam block every now and then to stop it sticking to the block. If the vein of the leaf is too thin, add a few more wisps of green wool. Repeat this process to make the side veins that branch off the central vein.

7

For the stem of the leaf, add a little lime green wool to the base of the central vein together with a few wisps of chestnut brown wool, then stab a few times with the single needle to secure it to the leaf. Continue to stab below the leaf so that the excess begins to mould together to form the stem. Roll the stem between your fingers and stab once more with the needle. This will create a smooth, dense finish. Put the leaf aside for later.

8

For the acorn, take a small amount of caramel wool and place it on the foam block to form a rectangle shape measuring roughly 2¾ x 1¼in (7 x 3cm). Stab a few times with the needle, lift it off the foam block, then, taking the wide end, roll the rectangle up tightly to form a small sausage shape and stab with the needle to secure.

9

Next, stab in the loose wispy ends with the needle so that the sausage forms the shape of a small egg. Roll the egg shape between the palms of your hands to smooth it. Place it on the foam block and stab all over once more with the needle to create a solid little egg shape measuring roughly ½in (1.5cm) long.

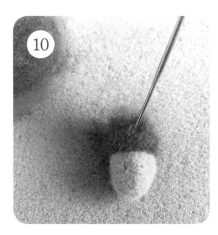

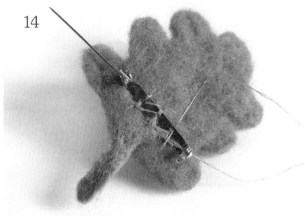

10

To create the acorn cap, place a small amount of chestnut brown wool on top of the egg shape and stab it in so that it starts covering the top and down the sides. Stop just above the halfway mark so that only the top is covered. Add more brown wool and start working it with the needle to create a domed shape. As you add a little more brown wool, begin to flatten the top so that it forms the characteristic shape of an acorn cap.

11

Now you need to make a little stem that sits on top; this will also help attach the acorn to the leaf. Take a small amount of brown wool measuring roughly $1^1/_4$ x $^3/_4$in (3 x 2cm), place it on the foam block and stab it a few times with the needle. Lift it off the foam block and roll it lengthways between your fingers to form a very thin sausage shape. Stab with the needle again a few times to give the stem a dense texture but leaving the ends wispy.

12

To attach the stem to the acorn, place one of the wispy ends on the top of the acorn cap. With the needle, stab in the wispy bits of wool around the outer edge of the stem until it adheres to the cap.

13

Position the other wispy end of the acorn stem on top of the oak leaf stem. Then, placing the whole piece on the foam block, stab in the wispy bits of the wool so that they attach to each other. Roll the end of the stem between your fingers and then give the stem a few more stabs with the needle.

14

Finally, using the sewing needle and some green thread, sew a brooch back to the reverse of the oak leaf, securing with a knot. Neaten off any stray threads.

Pumpkin Patch

Create your very own pumpkin patch with this needle-felted interpretation of a seasonal classic. You might find your patch grows bigger each year!

You will need

- Carded wool in white, orange, dark orange, light khaki, caramel and chestnut brown

- Polystyrene balls 4³⁄₄in (12cm) in diameter

- Single 38-gauge felting needle

- Multi-needle felting tool with six 38-gauge needles

- Blending tool

- Felting foam block or thick upholstery foam

- Pencil or pen

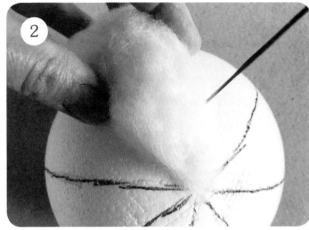

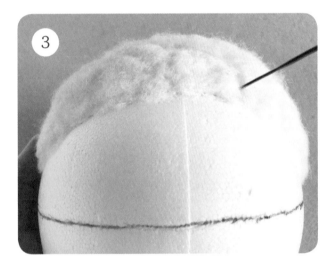

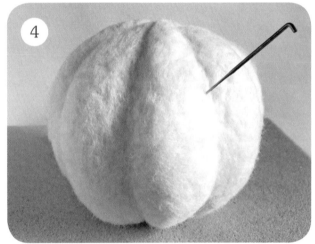

1

Take one of the 4³/₄in (12cm) polystyrene balls. With a pencil or pen, mark where the top and bottom are. Then draw a line from the top all the way around to the bottom and back up to the top on the other side. Repeat the process by drawing between the first line again from the top to the bottom and back up the other side. You should have a ball that looks as if it has been quartered vertically. Finally, draw lines between each of those lines so that the ball has eight sections.

2

Take a large amount of white wool measuring about 4³/₄ x 2in (12 x 5cm). Place the wool on the foam block and, using the single needle, stab all over it a few times. Take this felted section and place it at the top of one of the eight sections drawn in step 1. Stab it a few times with the needle and gently pull the wool down to the bottom of the ball. Next, stab with the single needle all over so that the wool adheres to the polystyrene ball and sits within the lines drawn.

3

Once the section has been filled, add some more white wool to the middle to raise the area. Start by using the multi-needle tool, as this will speed up the process, then use the single needle for definition. Repeat steps 2–3 using the same techniques to fill out the section opposite the first one.

4

Continue to repeat steps 2–3 to fill in the remaining sections of the pumpkin, adding more wool to areas that need plumping out and alternating between the single needle and the multi-needle tool.

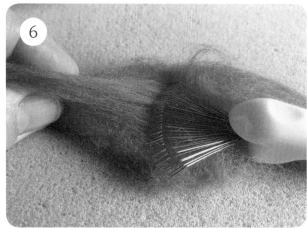

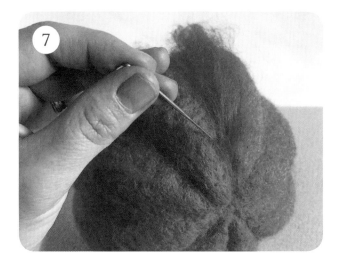

5

To add colour to the pumpkin, take some orange wool from the roving and start covering each section, stabbing in big wisps as you go using the single needle. Once you are happy with the first layer, go over it with the multi-needle tool, adding further wisps of orange wool where needed.

6

Next, add some tone and colour variation: take a big wisp of orange wool and lay a small amount of the darker orange wool over the top, then place them on the foam block. Holding one end with your fingers, use the blending tool to blend the colours by brushing the wool with downward strokes a few times.

7

Once you are happy that the wool has blended well, place the wool at the base of the pumpkin and in between one of the ridge sections and stab with the single needle to secure it in position. Continue to add more variation in colour in this way so that the pumpkin has some depth.

8

For the top of the pumpkin, start adding wisps of light khaki wool. Use the single needle to blend it into the ridges and all the way into the central top part of the pumpkin. Add wisps of orange wool to blend the edges of the light khaki wool so it doesn't look too harsh.

Use different sizes of polystyrene balls and change the shape of the pumpkin by adding extra wool.

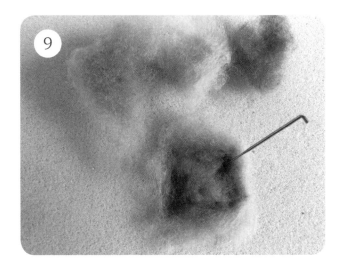

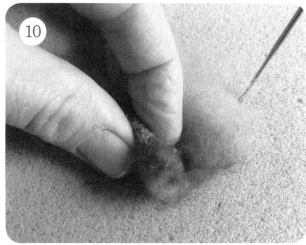

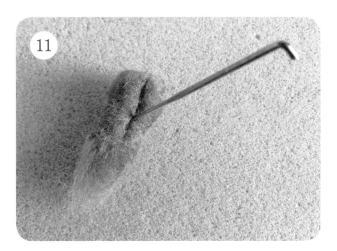

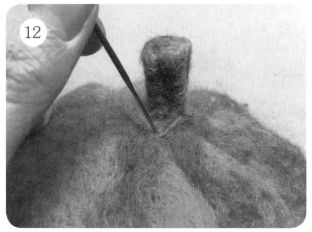

9

Next, make the stem of the pumpkin. Take a small amount of caramel wool, place it on the foam block and shape it into a square measuring roughly 2 x 2in (5 x 5cm). Place a light wispy layer of light khaki wool over the top and then another wisp of chestnut brown. Using the single needle, stab all over the square to secure the colours together. Lift the square off the foam block and turn over, then stab once more.

10

Roll the square to form a tight, fat sausage shape and stab all over to secure. Carry on stabbing the stem so that it becomes denser in texture and the colours have blended. Then stab one end to flatten off, leaving the other end wispy.

11

Once you are happy with the density and shape of the stem, stab with the single needle from the top to the base to create a vertical line. Enhance the line by stabbing with the needle a few times, repeating the process roughly four more times around the stem.

12

Place the stem on top of the pumpkin where you have already added some light khaki wool. With the wispy end of the stem touching the top, start stabbing with the single needle so that it adheres to the body of the pumpkin. Add more wisps of light khaki wool if needed, and blend in. Make further pumpkins using the other polystyrene balls as the base, varying the shapes and colours.

Holly Sprig

This felt version of cheerful holly leaves with bright red berries is perfect for embellishing picture frames, adorning festive dinner tables, personalizing gifts or even wearing as a brooch.

You will need

- Carded wool in forest green, spring green and flame red
- Sewing thread in green and red
- 2³⁄₄in (7cm) of red and white gingham ribbon
- Single 38-gauge felting needle
- Felting foam block or upholstery foam
- Scissors
- Sewing needle

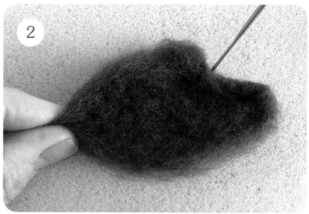

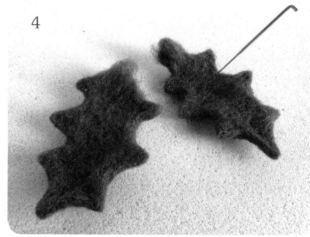

1

Take a large amount of forest green wool and pull it into a big loop to resemble a large leaf shape. Holding the wispy ends in one hand, place the leaf shape on the foam block and stab it all over with the single needle. Gently tease the leaf off the foam block and turn it over. Repeat the stabbing process a few more times, turning the leaf over every now and then. The leaf shape will reduce in size and become denser in texture. Add small wisps of forest green wool to any areas that may need it.

2

Now shape the characteristic spiky edges of the leaf by stabbing a slight curve at the side of the leaf near the top end.

3

Repeat this on the other side opposite the first curve so a point starts to form at the top of the leaf. Now stab another set of curves below the first set, creating two more spiky points.

4

Create two further curves to the leaf below the last set. Stab with the needle all the way around the outside edge of the leaf to accentuate its shape, leaving the wispy end unworked. Repeat steps 1–4 to create another holly leaf.

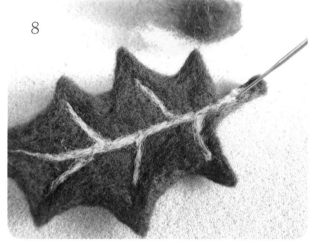

5

Now make the veins in the leaves. Take one of the leaves and place it on the foam block. Take a wisp of spring green wool and place it at the tip of the leaf, then stab with the needle a few times in the same spot. With the needle still stabbed into the leaf, pull the spring green wool with the other hand so that it creates a line that goes down the centre of the leaf. Stab with the needle along the line to secure it in position. Add more spring green wool to the line to achieve a stronger colour. Leave the wispy end you are holding for a later step.

6

Repeat the process in step 5 to create the side veins that run off the central vein. Turn the leaf over and very lightly stab any wispy bits of spring green wool that may have come through to the reverse.

7

Once you have finished the veins on the holly leaf, stab once more all the way around the outer edges to make them stand out. Roll the tips of the points between your fingers to make them look even more spiky.

8

To finish off the final part of the leaf, add a small amount of forest green and spring green wool to the wispy end of the holly leaf. Stab with the single needle to secure them together, then roll the end between your fingers to form a small stem. Continue stabbing with the needle to form its shape. Repeat steps 5–8 to finish off the other leaf.

Add hooks or hanging loops to the back to turn the leaves into tree decorations.

11

12

9

Now make the berries. Take a small amount of flame red wool and pull it into a small balloon shape. While holding the wispy ends in one hand, place the balloon shape on the foam block and stab it all over with the single needle.

10

Keep stabbing with the needle while rotating the balloon shape until it reduces in size. Then stab in the wispy bits that you are holding so that the shape becomes a small ball. To speed up the process and to reduce the ball in size, roll it between the palms of your hands while squeezing at the same time. Repeat the process to make a further two berries, then put them aside.

11

Now it is time to put all the components together. First, take one of the holly leaves and place it on top of the other at an angle. Thread the sewing needle with green thread, knot one end and sew through the top part of both leaves to secure them to each other, then fasten off the thread at the back. Take the piece of gingham ribbon and tie it around the stem, tie the ribbon into a bow and cut a V-shape at the ends.

12

The final step is to add the berries. Take the sewing needle and red thread, tie a knot at one end and sew through the holly leaves just under the bow to the front. Thread one of the berries on to the needle and sew back through both the berry and the leaves. Repeat this to sew the remaining berries around the first one, then sew back through to the reverse of the leaves and fasten off.

Snowman

Build on the techniques you have already learned to make this friendly snowman, complete with hat, scarf and tiny carrot nose, to add to your winter decorations.

You will need

- Carded wool in white, black, orange, sunflower yellow and red
- Single 38-gauge felting needle
- Multi-needle felting tool with six 38-gauge needles
- Felting foam block or thick upholstery foam

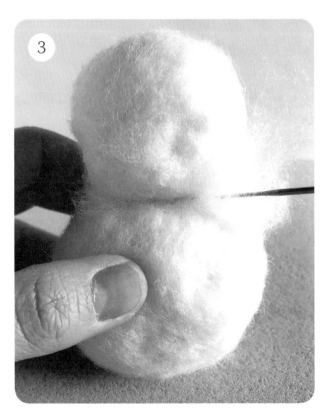

1

First, make the base of the snowman's body. Take a large amount of white wool and pull it into a balloon shape. While holding the wispy ends in one hand, place the balloon shape on the foam block. Stab it with the single needle a few times, rotating the balloon as you go. It will start to reduce in size and become denser, forming a small ball shape.

2

Turn the ball over and stab the wispy ends into the ball with the single needle. Continue to stab all over with the multi-needle tool, then roll the ball between the palms of your hands. The ball should be dense in texture and about 2³⁄₄in (7cm) in diameter. Put the ball aside.

3

Repeat steps 1–2 to make another ball for the top of the snowman's body, but using less wool, so that it ends up about 2in (5cm) in diameter. Place this ball on top of the first ball, adding wisps of white wool where they meet. Stab in the wisps of wool so that the two balls attach to each other. Repeat all the steps to make a smaller ball about 1¹⁄₄in (3cm) in diameter: this will be the snowman's head. Fix this in the same way to the top of the body.

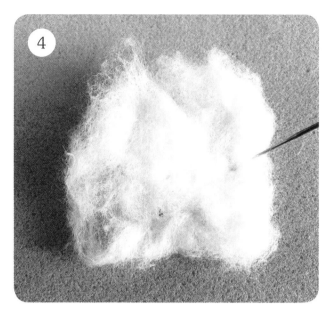

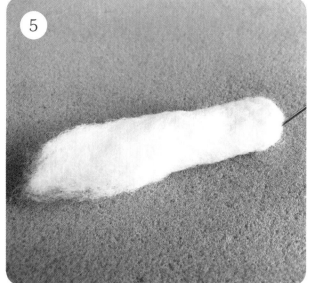

4

After you have made the snowman's body and head, add wisps of white wool all over the piece, stabbing with the single needle as you go. You want to end up with a smooth, soft-looking finish without hard edges. Next, take a small amount of white wool, place it on the foam block, and form a rectangle that measures roughly 3¼ x 2in (8 x 5cm). Stab all over the rectangle with the single needle, then gently tease it off the foam block.

5

Roll the rectangle into a tight sausage and stab it with the single needle to hold its shape. Continue stabbing all over the sausage, then roll it between the palms of your hands. Place it back on the foam block and stab all over once more. Next, stab at one end to round off the tip to create one of the snowman's arms. Repeat the process to make another arm.

6

Place one of the arms to the side of the snowman at the top of the second ball. Stab the wispy end of the arm with the single needle so that it adheres to the body, then stab all around the outside edge, adding wisps of white wool as you go. Repeat this process for the other arm, placing it so that the ends of the two arms touch each other.

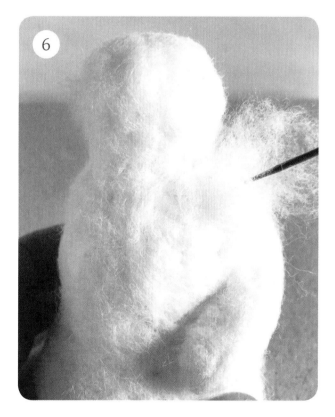

7

For the snowman's hat, take a small amount of black wool, place it on the foam block, and shape it roughly into a 2¹⁄₄in (6cm) circle with your hands. Using the single needle, stab all over, starting from the outer edge and working your way into the centre. Tease the circle off the foam block, turn it over, then stab again so that the circle eventually shrinks in size to about 1¹⁄₄in (3cm) in diameter. Lift it off the foam block every now and then, turning it over in between stabbing. Put the circle to one side for a later step, as this will form the base of a hat.

8

For the top part of the hat, take some black wool, form it into a rectangle roughly 1¹⁄₂ x 2¹⁄₄in (4 x 6cm), then place it on the foam block. Stab with the single needle all over, then lift it off the foam block and roll it lengthways into a tight sausage shape. Stab it with the single needle to hold its shape. Continue stabbing the sausage until it shrinks to about half its original size and becomes dense. Then flatten one end by stabbing in the wisps. While the piece is on the foam block, place the other wispy end of the sausage on top of the circle made in step 7 and carefully stab in the wisps with the needle. It should start resembling a top hat.

9

Place the hat on top of the snowman's head and stab with the single needle all the way around the base where the tall part of the hat meets the circular base. If you have trouble attaching the hat to the head, add small wisps of black wool as you stab.

10

For the details on the snowman's face, start by making a very small rectangle of orange wool and place it on the foam block. Stab it a few times with the single needle, then lift it off the foam block and roll it between your fingers so that it forms a very small sausage. Stab with the needle again, paying particular attention to one end, then pinch that end with your fingers to form a point; it should start looking like a tiny carrot. Position the thick end of the carrot onto the front of the snowman's head and lightly stab with the needle around the edge until the carrot is attached.

11

Take a wisp of black wool and place it on the snowman's face just above and to one side of the carrot nose. Stab in the same spot with the needle a few times so that the wool goes into the head. Next, wind the remaining wisps of black wool around the tip of the needle and stab it back into the

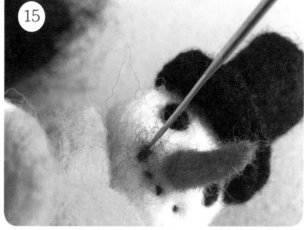

head to form an eye. Repeat this on the other side of the carrot to make the snowman's other eye. Add more wool if you want to make the eyes bigger.

12
Next comes the snowman's scarf. Take a strip of yellow wool and place it on the foam block. Stab it all over to form a rectangle measuring 5¹/₂ x ³/₄in (14 x 2cm). Gently tease the rectangle off the foam block and turn it over. Continue stabbing all over so it begins to shrink in size and resembles a scarf.

13
Wrap the scarf around snowman's neck with the ends crossing over just above the arms. Using the single needle, stab in to the scarf all the way around the outer and inner edges so that it attaches to the body, leaving the ends loose as if they are flapping in the wind. Now take a small

wisp of black wool and, using the same techniques for the eyes, make some small black spots on the snowman's body for the buttons.

14
Using a small amount of red wool, place a wisp directly above the rim of the hat and stab in one spot a few times with the single needle. Then pull the wool with the other hand around the rim to form a red stripe and stab the wool with the needle to secure.

15
Finally, to give the snowman a cheeky smile, stab in some very small wisps of black wool using the technique in step 11 to create a few black dots for the mouth.

Advanced

Adonis Blue Butterfly

In this more advanced project, I recreated the beautiful colours of the Adonis blue butterfly. You could adapt this to create the butterfly of your choice or feature your favourite colours.

You will need

- Pure carded wool in cornflower blue, baby blue, turquoise, white, black and mouse grey
- Multi-needle felting tool with six 38-gauge needles
- Single 38-gauge felting needle
- Felting foam block or thick upholstery foam
- Square box frame for display

1

To start the butterfly, make the wings. For the two top wings, take a piece of cornflower blue wool measuring roughly 2¼in (6cm) high by 1½in (4cm) wide. Mould it with your hands into the shape of a wing with a rounded edge towards the wider part. Over the top, layer a smaller piece of baby blue wool. Place it at the rounded bottom edge of the wing, with a smaller piece of turquoise wool just above. Do the same for the second wing to create a mirror image. Using the multi-needle tool, stab all over. Gently tease the wing off the foam block, turn it over and stab once more. Then add a small amount of white wool along the bottom, rounded edge of the wing. Stab it with the single needle to create a clean band along the edge. Repeat the process for the second wing. You will find that using the multi-needle tool will blend the colours neatly together.

2

Now shape and smooth the edge of the wing. With one hand, roll over the edge and stab it with the single needle to secure it in place. Using the same technique, work your way

all around the outer edge of the wing, leaving the thinner end wispy and unworked. Repeat the steps to shape the other wing using the first as a guide.

3

Next, add some pattern to the wings. Take a small amount of black wool. With the single needle, stab a wisp of it halfway down the outer edge of the thinner end of the wing. Stab a few times in the same spot, then, with the other hand, gently pull to create a line down the outer edge. Stab with the needle along the line to secure it in place, taking it all the way around the curved end and stopping at the point where the wing straightens. Repeat the process to make the line stronger in colour if necessary.

4

Using the same technique, add five fine black lines that extend into the white fringe of the wing. Repeat these steps for the other wing, using the original as a mirror image.

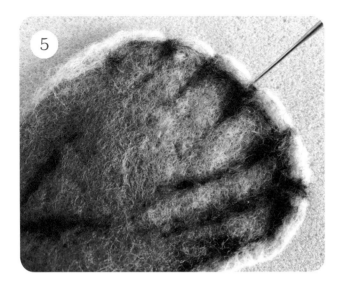

5

After adding the pattern, create a scalloped edge to the rounded end of the wings. Stab the single needle in one place a few times on the rounded edge to create a small dent. Repeat this process a couple of centimetres along and at least five more times to create the scalloped effect. Finally, stab small wisps of black wool into the dented areas. Repeat these steps for the remaining wing, mirroring the pattern. Put the wings aside for later.

6

Once you have completed the butterfly's top wings, it is time to make the larger bottom wings. Take a larger piece of the cornflower blue wool, measuring roughly 2¾in (7cm) high by 2in (5cm) wide. Mould it with your hands into a wider wing shape, then lay small amounts of baby blue and turquoise over the top as in step 1. Stab it all over using the multi-needle tool. Gently tease the wing off the foam block, turn it over and stab once more. Then add some white wool along the rounded end as in step 1. Follow step 2 to shape and smooth the edges. Repeat the same technique to create the other wing so that they mirror each other.

7

Now add the detail to these set of wings. Follow steps 3 and 4 to create five fine black lines at the rounded end. Using the same technique, add three lines in baby blue wool so that they fan out from the thinner end of the wing.

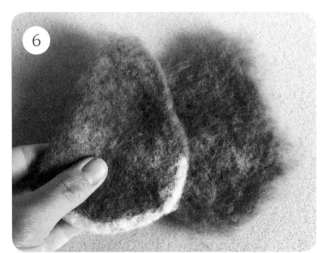

When making the second wing of a pair, place a mirror next to the first wing to use as a guide when repeating the pattern on the other wing.

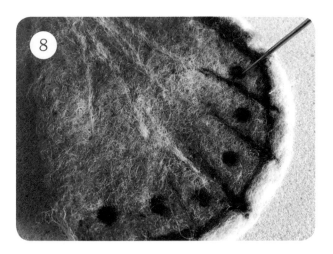

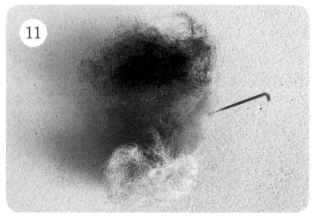

8

For the final detail, create the black dots that sit in between the black lines. Using the single needle, place a wisp of black wool in between the first two lines, then stab in the same spot a few times so that the wisps create a dot shape. Any loose wisps can be secured by entwining them around the needle and stabbing them in place. Repeat the process so that you end up with six dots sitting between the black lines. Add the scalloped edge detail by following step 5. Repeat all the processes to create the details on the other wing.

9

Now join the wings together. Take the two larger bottom wings and overlap the thinner wispy unworked ends. Using the multi-needle tool, stab over the unworked areas to join them together. Tease the wings off the foam block, turn over and repeat the process to the reverse. Turn them right side up on the foam block once more.

10

Place the two smaller wings on top of the bottom wings so that the unworked ends cross. Gently stab with the single needle to secure all four wings together, then put aside.

11

To make the body of the butterfly, take a small amount of cornflower blue wool. Place a few wisps of black wool and mouse grey wool at the top and bottom, to form a rectangle measuring roughly $3^{1}/_{2}$ x $4^{1}/_{4}$in (9 x 11cm). Stab all over with the single needle to flatten it. Then lift it carefully off the foam block, turn it over and stab with the needle once more. Roll the strip tightly lengthways to form a thin sausage shape. Stab with the needle to secure the shape, leaving the ends unworked. Roll the sausage between the palms of your hands, then stab once more to create a tight, solid sausage shape. Finally, stab in the unworked ends with the needle to give the sausage shape rounded tips.

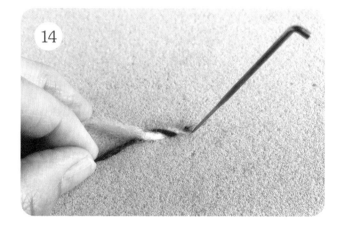

Make several butterflies and turn them into a mobile by stringing them on dowelling rods or you could make smaller versions and turn them into brooches.

12

Now shape the body. Start adding wisps of black wool to the black-tipped end of the sausage. Stab with the needle to fatten up this end. Then, about ½in (1.5cm) from the top, stab in either side to create the head, twisting the end between your fingers to help make it smaller. Add rounded bits of black wool either side of the head to create eyes for the butterfly.

13

Once you have made the basic body shape, you need to connect it to the wings. Place the body in the middle of the wings that were joined together in step 10. Place the body so that the head sits proud about ⅜in (1cm) above the top wings. With the single needle, stab below the head in a line. Following that, stab at the base of the body all the way around, then turn over and stab the reverse in a vertical line. Turn the butterfly back over. Where the body starts getting fatter, stab with the needle across the body to create a line. Go over that line a few times, as this helps to attach the body to the wings. Repeat this process ⅜in (1cm) below

the first line a further four times to make a ribbed effect on the butterfly's abdomen. Add wisps of black wool below the top wings nearest the abdomen to add definition.

14

Now make the butterfly's antennae. Take a small amount of black wool, pull it into a fine wisp and roll it between the palms of your hands to form a string-like effect. Take a small amount of white wool and repeat this process. Hold the two pieces of wool 'string' together and stab one end with the single needle so that they are fixed, then twist this to create a striped effect. Finally, stab a few times up and down the whole piece with the single needle and repeat the process of rolling it between your hands. By repeating this step several times you will end up with a denser felted piece. Then stab with the needle in the middle to form a V-shape. Lastly, position the antennae at the back of the head so the V-shape points up. Place a wisp of black wool at the base where it sits on the head and stab with the single needle to secure it in place. Once you have finished making the butterfly, place it in the box frame and display it on the wall.

Rabbit

This sweet little rabbit has an adorable expression and will sit perfectly in the palm of your hand. Make him some companions in a variety of colours to produce a whole warren of bunnies.

You will need

- Pure carded wool in mouse grey, white, pale pink and black
- Wensleydale wool curls in cream/white
- 1/4in (6mm) shiny black beads for eyes
- Black and white sewing thread
- Ribbon for a bow
- Multi-needle felting tool with six 38-gauge needles
- Single 38-gauge felting needle
- Felting foam block or thick upholstery foam
- Sewing needle

1

To make the body, take a thick strip of grey wool, roughly 4 x 4³/₄in (10 x 12cm). Place it on the foam block and stab with the multi-needle tool a few times. Tease it off the foam block, turn it over and roll it into a thick sausage shape with a slightly fatter end. Stab lightly with the single needle all over to secure, rounding off the fatter end and leaving the other end unworked for attaching the head later.

2

For the head, take a smaller amount of grey wool and make a balloon shape. Holding the end with one hand, stab all over, rotating as you go, leaving the bit you are holding as a loose fluffy end.

3

To join the head to the body, place the head on top of the body and stab the loose ends together. For the paws, take four equal strips of grey wool roughly 2¹/₄ x 2³/₄in (6 x 7cm). For the front paws, flatten the surface of two of the strips by stabbing with the single needle. Lift the strips off the foam block, turn over and stab once again. Then roll each piece tightly lengthways to form a thin sausage shape. Stab all over, leaving the ends unworked, then roll between the palms of your hands and stab all over again. This will create a dense, smooth finish. Add a wisp of white wool at one end of each sausage and stab with the needle to form a rounded tip. This will become the paw of the rabbit. Do the same to the final two strips of grey wool for the back legs. Make the rounded tip ends slightly fatter by adding a bit of grey wool in that area.

4

Now shape the legs and paws. For the two front paws, stab a line about ³/₁₆in (5mm) from the rounded end to mark the angle of the paw. Stab above that line, then roll that area between your fingers to form an ankle. Turn the paw over so the angled bit rests on the edge of the foam block and stab the base of the paw flat. Repeat for the other leg.

5

For the back legs, the paws need to be longer and flatter. Start forming the ankle line higher, roughly ³/₈in (1cm) from the tip. Add more grey wool to widen and shape the paw if needs be, remembering to stab the base of the paw using the edge of the foam.

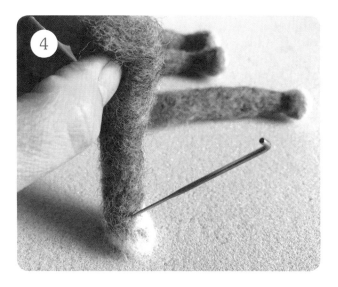

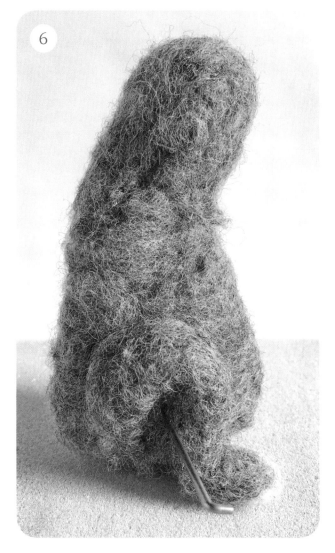

6

To attach the back legs to the body, bend the leg to form
the arch of the knee, place on the side of the main body and
stab with the needle all over to hold in place. Add wisps of
grey wool to fix key areas in place. Once both back legs are
attached to the sides, place the front paws in between the
back legs on the front of the body. Stab the needle into the
wispy ends to fix them in place.

7

Gradually add more grey wool over the back legs to create
the rabbit's hip and rump, stabbing repeatedly as you go.
For the front legs and the chest of the rabbit, start adding
some white wool along with the grey to blend and build
out the chest.

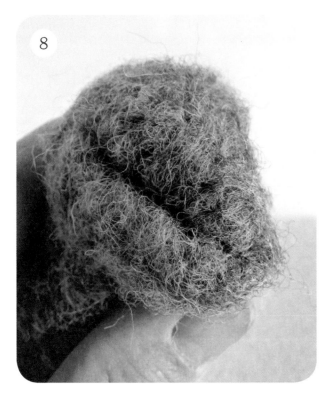

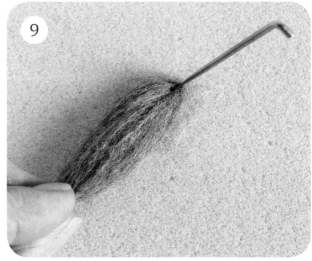

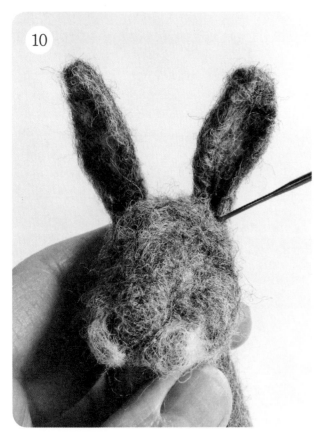

8

To start creating the shape of the face and nose structure, make a small loose ball with an unworked end, similar to that in step 2, about a third of the size of the head. Join it to the front of the head with the single needle, adding wisps of grey wool to the sides and ridge of the nose. Once covered with wool, stab a V-shaped line with the needle to the tip of the nose. This will act as a guide to where the eyes will sit and shape the rest of the face. Now stab a smaller upside-down V-line just under to form the mouth. Add small lumps of grey wool either side of the mouth to create cheeks. The more you stab with the needle, the denser the texture will become. If needs be, add more wool with a little white blended in. At the top of the V, start stabbing the needle to make indentations for the eye sockets. Add more wool if you find it sinking in too far.

9

To make the ears, pull a small length of grey wool into a loop shape. Holding the ends in one hand, stab with the single needle on one side, then turn the piece over and repeat. As you stab, the loop will shrink and become denser. Shape the pointed end by rubbing the tip between your fingers, then stab the point into a rounded edge. Repeat the same process for the other ear.

10

Blend light wisps of pink and white to the inside of each ear before fixing them in place onto the head by stabbing in the grey wispy ends on the sides. Add a few wisps of grey to the base of the ears where they meet the head.

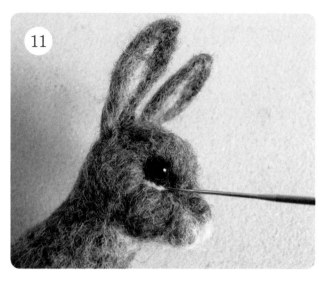

11

Now make the detail on the face. With the sewing needle and black thread, sew the two beads into position where you made the indentations earlier. Fasten off the loose thread and hide it within the head. Add touches of black wool around the outside of the beads to give more depth, then add a small amount of white wool just under the eye. For the nose, stab in a small amount of pink blended with white to form an upside-down triangle. For the mouth and outer edges of the nose, stab in a wispy bit of black, following the line you shaped earlier. Sew on some white thread for whiskers, remembering to knot the end.

12

Finally, make a fluffy white tail. Take a small amount of the curly Wensleydale wool. Place it at the back of the rabbit's bottom and stab in place with a wisp of white wool. You can shape it into a rough ball shape. Add a ribbon around the neck and tie into a bow.

You could use different colours of wool and add fluffy curls to add texture.

Bumblebee

Nearly everyone loves bees, both for their distinctive yellow and black stripes and their industrious ways. This advanced project makes a larger-than-life bumblebee that you can actually stroke!

You will need

- Pure carded wool in black, sunflower yellow and white
- 6 x 6in (15 x 15cm) piece of white voile fabric
- Beading wire
- Wire cutters
- 5/16in (8mm) black beads
- Black sewing thread
- Single 38-gauge felting needle
- Felting foam block or thick upholstery foam
- Sewing needle
- Scissors

You can use many of the techniques in this project to create all types of bugs.

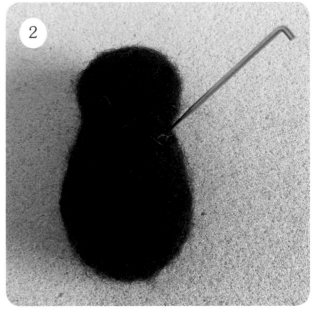

1

Start with the bumblebee body. Take a large, thick piece of black wool and shape it into rectangle roughly measuring 5 1/2 x 2 3/4in (14 x 7cm). Place it on the foam block, and using the single needle, stab the piece all over. Lift the rectangle off the foam and turn it over, then stab with the needle all over once more. Roll the rectangle widthways into a tight sausage shape, stabbing in the loose edges to secure while keeping both ends wispy.

2

To shape the body, start stabbing with the needle at one end to round it off slightly, then stab the sides more to make it pointed. Add more black wool to that area to fatten this section, as this will form the main part of the body. After that, start stabbing lightly about 2in (5cm) up from the pointed end all the way around to create an indentation. Round off that end by stabbing with the needle.

3

Next, take a small amount of black wool and create a small ball with an unworked end by pulling it into a loop. Holding the wispy ends with one hand, stab all over while rotating the piece. Attach the ball to the bee's body by placing the wispy ends of the ball to the smaller rounded end, then stab with the needle to secure it in place. Place a few more wisps of black wool over this area to hide any joins that may show; this will form the bee's head. To shape the area where the eyes will go, use the single needle to stab either side of the ball a few times to create indentations for later. Put the body aside.

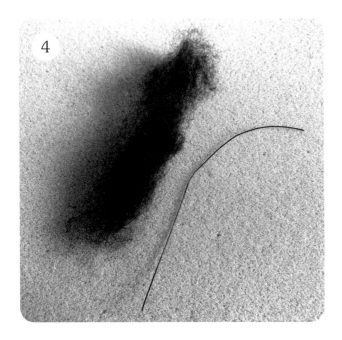

4

Now make the bee's legs. Take a thin strip of black wool roughly 4in (10cm) long. Place it on the foam block and stab all over with the single needle. Gently tease the wool off the foam block and turn it over. Then take a piece of beading wire slightly shorter than the length of the wool and place it along one edge lengthways. Roll the wool tightly to form a very thin sausage with the wire encased. Stab all over so the piece holds its shape, leaving the ends wispy.

5

Once the wire has been covered, bend it in half to form a V-shape. Roll it between your fingertips and stab with the needle to neaten off the tips. Next, take a very small wisp of yellow wool, place it about $^3/_8$in (1cm) up from one tip end and stab with a needle all the way around the sausage to form a yellow line. Repeat this on the other side so that it mirrors the effect. Then, with black wool, do the same a further $^3/_8$in (1cm) up so that the legs begin to get thicker the closer you get to the middle of the V. Finally, add another strip of yellow wool $^3/_8$in (1cm) above the last lot of black wool. Again, repeat to the other side of the V. You should end up with a striped V-shaped set of legs. Repeat the process to make a further two sets.

6

Now attach the legs to the underside of the bee's body. Start by taking one set of legs and position it so that the V-part sits in between the head and the first section of the body. Take a wisp of black wool and place it over the middle part of the legs. Stab with the single needle to secure the legs to the body. Add more wool if needed and bend the legs to give the bee some knees. Next, place another set of legs at the beginning of the larger part of the body. Use the same process to attach these legs. Place the final set of legs just after these and attach them to the body in the same way. Once they are set in place, bend the legs back away from the head.

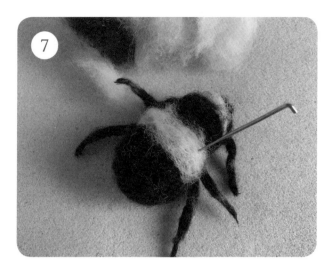

7

Now add some colour. Take a wisp of yellow wool and place it on the body just behind the head. Using the single needle, stab it in so it blends and follows the shape around to form a stripe. Repeat this process but move up to the second part of the bee's body, so the bee has its familiar yellow stripes. Once you have done that, add white wool to the bee's pointed bottom, stabbing in with the needle to secure it in place.

8

To create the body's fluffy texture, take a strip of yellow wool that is the width of the first yellow stripe. Place it over one of the yellow edges and stab with the single needle a few times in a line along the width so that it follows the round shape of the body. Repeat the process on the other side of the yellow strip so you end up with four rows of fluffy yellow wool sticking up.

9

With scissors, trim the four yellow rows of wool to just above the body to create the bumblebee's fluffy texture. Follow step 8 to create the other yellow stripe on the head and the white pointed bottom of the bee, then trim as above to create the fluffy texture.

10

For the wings, take the voile fabric, fold it in half and cut out the shape of a bee's wing to fit the size of your bee; you should end up with two identical wings. To fix the wings to the body, place one of them on top of the first black stripe of the body. With a small wisp of black wool, stab into the base of the wing to secure it into position. When it is properly attached, repeat the process for the other wing, positioning it so they sit side by side.

11

Next, attach the eyes. Take the needle and thread, tie a double knot at one end and sew through one of the dents you made in step 3. Come out through the dent on the other side, pull on the thread to make sure it is secure, then place one of the beads on the thread and sew back through to the first dent. Once again, place a bead on the thread and carefully sew back through to the first bead. Tie a knot around that bead and make sure it is tight and secure, then fasten off and hide the thread within the head of the bee.

12

Finally, make the bee's antennae. Take a small amount of black wool, pull it into a fine wisp and roll it between the palms of your hands to form a string-like effect. Place the 'string' on the foam block and stab up and down a few times with the single needle, lifting it off the foam block every now and then. Roll it one more time between your fingers until you are happy with the thickness. Then bend it in half and place it on the bee's head above the eyes. Take a small amount of black wool and stab the wisps in with the needle to secure the antennae in place.

If you don't have any voile fabric, make the wings by shaping two pieces of white wool into petal shapes.

Sleeping Fox

The beautiful fox is often spotted, both in the countryside and increasingly in urban areas. The techniques used to make this sleepy fellow will help you go on and make many more adorable creatures.

You will need

- Carded wool in chestnut brown, brickwork brown, caramel, cream and black
- Wensleydale wool locks in cream
- ¼in (6mm) shiny beads for eyes
- Black sewing thread
- Single 38-gauge felting needle
- Multi-needle felting tool with six 38-gauge needles
- Blending tool
- Felting foam block or thick upholstery foam
- Sewing needle
- Scissors

1

To start making the body of the fox, take a large amount of chestnut brown wool and place it on the foam block. Shape it into a rectangle measuring roughly 4 x 6in (10 x 15cm). Place a few smaller wisps of brickwork brown wool over the top. Using the multi-needle tool, stab the rectangle a few times. Gently tease the rectangle off the foam block and turn it over, then stab once more with the multi-needle tool.

2

Next, roll the rectangle into a fairly tight sausage shape. Stab with the single needle to secure, leaving the ends wispy. Start curving the sausage shape while adding more wisps of chestnut brown wool at one end, raising the area and starting to create the backside of the fox.

3

To blend the colours, use the blending tool by stroking it in one direction down the chestnut brown and brickwork brown wool on the foam block while holding the two wisps in one hand. Add the blended bits to the raised area created in step 2 and use the single needle to sculpt and define the rear of the fox.

4

To make the head of the fox, pull a small handful of chestnut brown wool from the roving. With two hands, create a balloon shape. Then, holding the wispy ends with one hand, stab all over with the single needle until the balloon shape has become dense and about 1¼in (3cm) in size but with the ends you are holding still wispy.

5

Repeat this process with a smaller amount of chestnut wool to create a small ball. Attach this to the top of the bigger ball by stabbing in the wispy ends of the small ball with the single needle. This will form the structure for the fox's muzzle.

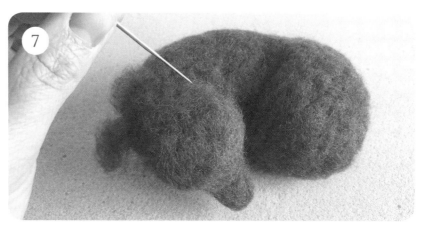

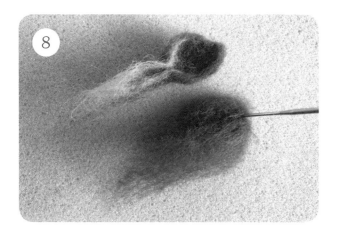

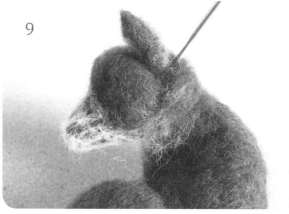

6

Start adding wisps of chestnut brown wool from the tip of the nose to the back of the head and gently stab them in with the single needle. This will start to hide any joins while at the same time shaping the muzzle. Add some more wool to either side of the muzzle; this will create cheeks and give some definition to the area. Make two indentations with the needle either side of the muzzle where the eyes will sit later.

7

Now attach the head by placing the wispy end at the unworked end of the body. With the single needle, start stabbing in the wisps, adding more wool as you go, creating the curve of the neck and strengthening it at the same time. Following that, place wisps of cream wool just under the chin of the fox, stabbing it in and working it down the neck slightly.

8

To make the ears, pull a small amount of chestnut brown wool into a loop that resembles the shape of an ear. Holding the wispy ends in one hand, place the piece on the foam block. Stab the piece with the single needle around the

outside, then gradually work your way into the centre. Lift the ear off the foam block and turn it over. Add a small amount of dark brown wool to the tip of the ear and a small amount of caramel wool to the wispy end. Then stab with the needle all over, lifting the ear off the foam block every now and then. As the ear starts to shrink in size, place the tip between your fingers and give it a gentle squeeze; this will give the fox's ear a pointed tip. Finally, stab the wisp at the base to give it a pinch. Repeat this process to create another ear.

9

Once you have made the ears, attach them to the head. Take one ear and place the wispy end on top of the head so it sits slightly to one side. With the single needle, stab in the wisps of wool so they blend into the back of the head and down towards the cheek. Add an extra-small wisp of chestnut wool to the base of the ear at the front and stab it in with the needle. Repeat this step for the other ear, adding more chestnut wool in between the ears to hide any joins.

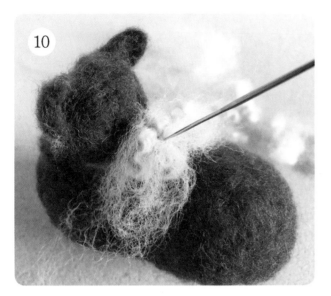

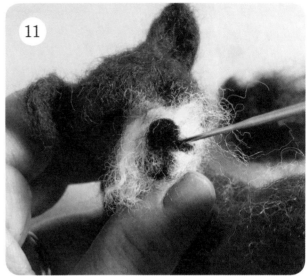

If you don't want to use beads for eyes, stab in a small amount of black wool instead.

10

Now add the features to the fox's face. First, take a lock of the Wensleydale wool and lay it across the top of the fox's muzzle. Then place a thin wisp of cream wool over the top. With the single needle, stab a line along the centre of the muzzle so that the layers become attached. Do this a few times, then gradually stab down the sides, stopping halfway. Once attached, trim the wool with scissors so that it remains slightly fluffy. Add a wisp of caramel to the top of the muzzle, then stab a few more times with the needle around the tip.

11

Next, take a small wisp of black wool, place it at the end of the fox's muzzle and stab in the same spot a few times. The black wool will start to create a small dot. With the last few wisps, wind it around the needle and stab it back into the same spot to create the nose. Just under the nose, place a small wisp of black wool and stab with the needle once. Then pull the wool down to one side to create a small line for the mouth. Stab the line with the needle to secure this, then do the same on the other side.

12

For the eyes, take the sewing needle and black thread and tie a knot at one end. Push the needle through one of the indentations made in step 6 and come back out through the other one, pulling the thread until it stops. Thread one of the beads onto the sewing needle and sew back through the indentation and out to the other side. Thread the other bead onto the same needle and push it through the indentation back out to the first bead. Knot the thread around that bead, push the sewing needle out to the back of the fox's head and cut off the excess thread.

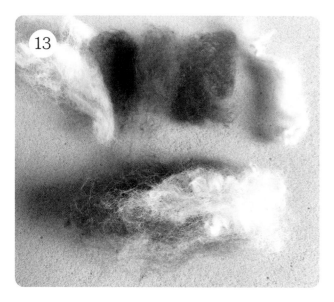

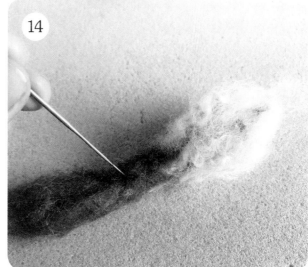

13

Finally, create the bushy tail. Take a piece of chestnut wool measuring 4 x 2in (10 x 5cm) and lay it on the foam block. Place a thin layer of dark brown wool over the top with a lock of the Wensleydale and a wisp of cream wool slightly sticking out. Stab with the single needle a few times to tie the layers together. Gently tease the piece off the foam block and turn it over to stab once more.

14

With the chestnut brown side facing down, roll the rectangle into a tight sausage shape and stab with the needle in the area that only holds the brown wool. Roll that bit of the tail between the palms of your hands, then stab it again so it becomes dense. Leave the curly white part of the tail still bushy. Place the brown wispy end of the tail to the rear end of the fox and stab in the wisps with the needle. Add extra wisps of chestnut wool blended with the dark brown wool to cover any joins above and under the fox. Finally, place the bushy end of the tail under the chin of the fox so that he looks as if he is sleeping.

Festive Wreath

Adorn your front door with a unique whimsical wreath complete with a cute needle-felted mouse. You will be the envy of the neighbourhood!

You will need

- Carded wool in mouse grey, white, red and dark grey
- 10in (25cm) polystyrene wreath ring
- Black sewing thread
- ¼in (6mm) shiny black beads for eyes
- 4in (10cm) of red ribbon
- Single 38-gauge felting needle
- Multi-needle felting tool with six 38-gauge needles
- Felting foam block or thick upholstery foam
- Sewing needle and thread

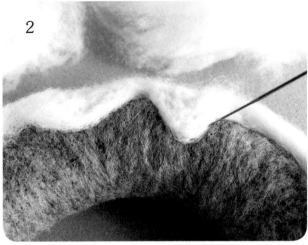

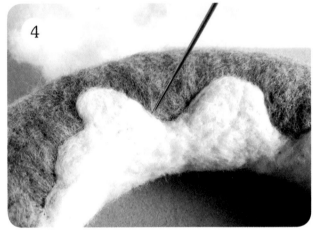

1

Take a large, thick piece of mouse grey wool and wrap it around part of the polystyrene wreath. Stab the wool in loosely with the single needle to attach it. Continue to attach more mouse grey wool to the rest of the wreath so it is completely covered and add wisps of wool to any areas with bare patches.

2

Once the wreath is covered, go over the whole piece with the multi-needle tool so that all the wool has adhered to the wreath. It should look and feel smooth, not fluffy. Next, take the white wool and lay a thick piece just on top of the wreath so that it drapes as if snow has just fallen. Use the single needle to stab it in, adding more wisps of white wool where it appears to be thin.

3

To create the thick patches of snow that hang over the edge, take a small amount of white wool and pull it into a petal-shaped loop. Place it directly onto the wreath over the mouse grey wool and blend it in to the white snowy area by stabbing it with the single needle.

4

When you have added enough snow, go over it with the multi-needle tool to give a smooth, even finish. Then, using the single needle, stab all the way around the outer edges of the snow to accentuate the detail. Repeat this process to add more snow to the lower inside edge of the wreath.

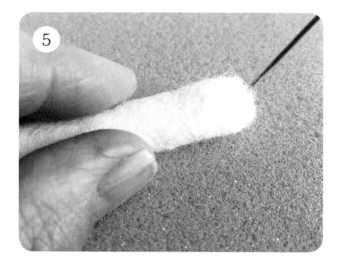

A wreath can be made for any time of the year; use other projects from this book to embellish the wreath.

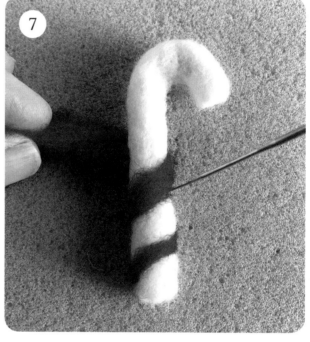

5

Now move onto the decorations. For the candy canes, take a piece of white wool roughly 3¼ x 2in (8 x 5cm) and place it on the foam block. Stab all over with the single needle, then tease is it off the foam block and roll it lengthways into a tight sausage shape. Stab with the needle all over the sausage to hold its shape, then roll it between the palms of your hands, squeezing it a little. Stab it once more all over, stabbing the ends to flatten them off.

6

Make a further four more little sausages, all the same size and width with flat ends. To make the curved shape at the end of the candy canes, start stabbing at one side about 1¼in (3cm) down from one end. It will start to bend as you stab. Continue stabbing and work your way back to the shorter end to create a curve. Stab either side of the curve and the sides to hold its shape. Once you have one finished, repeat the process with the remaining four canes.

7

Next, add the red stripe to the candy canes. Take a long wisp of red wool and stab it into one end of the cane lightly to secure it. Then pull the wool and wind it in a spiral pattern down the cane, stabbing the outer edge of the red stripe very lightly with the needle as you go until you reach the end. At the end, stab in the last bit of red wool, teasing off any excess. Add the red spiral stripe to the remaining candy canes and put them aside.

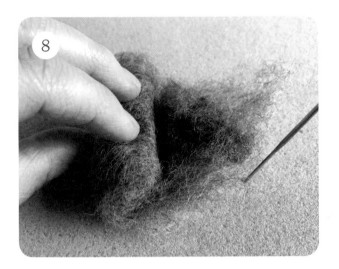

For an easier project, you could include a festive ornament instead of the mouse.

8

Now make the little mouse that will sit in the middle of the wreath. Take a small amount of dark grey wool roughly $1^1/_2$ x $2^1/_4$in (4 x 6cm), place it on the foam block, and stab all over with the single needle. Lift it off the foam and roll it into a sausage shape, stabbing with the needle to secure its shape. Stab in the wispy ends to round them off. Add more wisps of dark grey wool to fatten one end. Then add a small amount of dark grey wool at the other end to form a pointed nose for the mouse, rubbing the end between your fingers to make a point.

9

To create the ears for the mouse, pull a small amount of dark grey wool into a loop. Place it on the foam block and stab it with the single needle from the outside edge into the middle while holding the wispy ends in one hand. Lift the ear off the foam block, turn it over and stab again so that it shrinks in size. Add a small wisp of white wool in the centre of the ear and stab it in lightly. Repeat these steps to create the other ear, remembering to lift it off the block and turn it over every now and then.

10

Attach the ears to the top of the head by stabbing in the wispy ends of each ear with the needle, adding a wisp of dark grey wool to the front and in between the ears. Next, make an indentation with the needle either side of the pointy nose by stabbing in the same spot a few times. Then, with the sewing needle and black thread, sew a bead into each indentation for the eyes of the mouse. Knot the thread around the last bead and fasten off through the back of the mouse's head. For the tail, take a thin strip of dark grey wool, place it on the foam block and stab it a few times with the single needle. Tease it off the foam and roll it into a thin, tight, sausage shape. Then roll it between the palms of your hands, making one end pointed. Attach it to the base of the mouse by stabbing in the wispy end to the bottom of the body.

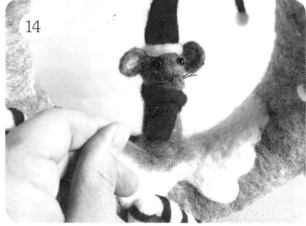

11

For the hat, shape a small amount of red wool into rough triangle. Place it on the foam block and stab all over with the single needle. Lift the triangle off the foam and roll it tightly into a cone. Stab it with the needle to secure its shape, then continue stabbing but rotating it as you go. Roll the thinner end between the palms of your hands to form a point, then add more red wool to the bottom of the cone to fatten the base. Next, stab one side of the cone towards the top to curl the end. Place the hat on the mouse's head between the ears, then stab a wisp of white wool around the base to attach the hat to the head. Finally, stab in a wisp of white wool to the tip of the hat, rolling it between your fingers to form a small ball.

12

Thread the sewing needle with some black thread, knot one end, then sew some whiskers on the end of the mouse's pointed nose. Now make the scarf. Take a strip of red wool measuring roughly $4^3/_4$ x $1^1/_4$in (12 x 3cm), place it on the foam block and stab the single needle all over it. Lift the piece off the foam, turn it over and stab around the outside edge, making it sharp and crisp. Wrap the red strip around the mouse's neck, crossing over at the front. Stab in the outer edges so that it adheres to the body and the neck.

13

Gather all the components together, then lay the wreath down on the table and place the candy canes at different angles on top. Make sure the gaps between them are roughly equal, and leave the top of the wreath free to attach the ribbon later. To attach the candy canes to the wreath, stab with the single needle through the canes, paying particular attention to where the cane touches the wreath.

14

Next, place the mouse sitting on the snow on the inside of the wreath. Add a wisp of dark grey wool around the base of its body. Stab the wisps of wool into the base and the mouse at the same time with the single needle so that the mouse adheres to the wreath. Finally, tie a length of red ribbon around the top of the wreath, tie it into a bow and hang the wreath up.

Polar Bear

Few of us will have the chance to see a polar bear in its natural habitat, so why not make your own cuddly needle-felted version?

You will need

- Carded wool in cream, dark grey and black
- ¼in (6mm) shiny beads for eyes
- Black sewing thread
- Multi-needle felting tool with six 38-gauge needles
- Single 38-gauge felting needle
- Felting foam block or thick upholstery foam
- Sewing needle

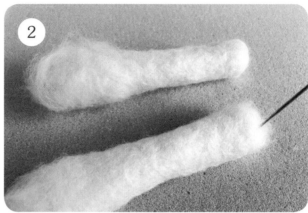
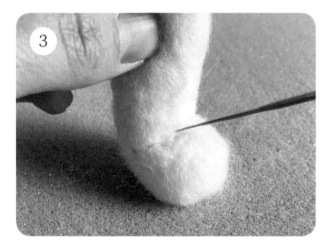
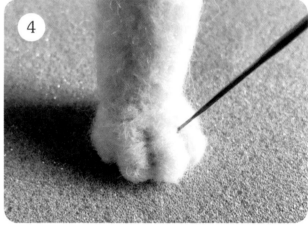

1

Start with the body. Take a large amount of cream wool and shape it into rectangle measuring roughly 4³/₄ x 6in (12 x 15cm). Place the rectangle on the foam block and stab all over the wool with the multi-needle tool. Lift the piece off the foam block and turn it over, then roll the rectangle widthways into a sausage shape. Stab the sausage with the single needle to hold its shape, leaving the ends wispy. Next, using the multi-needle tool, stab all over the sausage shape, rotating as you go. Stab one of the wispy ends to round it off. The sausage should remain slightly bouncy to the touch.

2

Now make the polar bear's legs. Take some cream wool and shape it into a rectangle measuring roughly 4 x 4³/₄in (10 x 12cm). Place it on the foam block. Stab all over it with the single needle, then turn it over and stab once more. Gently tease it off the foam block, then roll it into a tight sausage shape, stabbing with the needle to secure its shape but leaving the ends wispy. Roll the sausage between the

palms of your hands to speed up the process of making the piece denser in texture. Next, stab in one of the wispy ends to form a rounded tip. Repeat this step to make the other three legs all the same length.

3

Next, shape the polar bear's foot. Take one of the legs. Holding it upright, stab a line into the leg about ¹/₂in (1.5cm) up from the tip. The leg will naturally start to bend at this point. Stop stabbing when it does this, then stab above this line and squeeze the area between your fingertips to create the ankle.

4

Now make the claws. Stab a line in the bent section of the leg with the single needle to create the impression of a claw. Make a further three lines so that the foot looks as if it has four claws. You may need to go over the lines with the needle a few times.

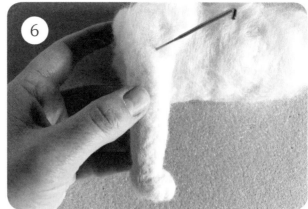

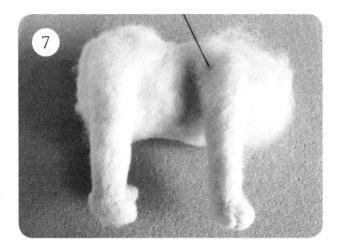

5

Once the claws have been created, turn the foot upside down and position it over the edge of the foam block so that the base of the claw is facing you. Stab the area with the single needle to flatten the base as well as highlighting the claws underneath. Repeat steps 3–5 to shape the feet and mark the claws on the other three legs.

6

Now attach the legs to the body. Place the large sausage shape made in step 1 onto the foam block. Take one of the legs and position it at the rounded end so that the wispy ends of the leg sit high on the body. Using the single needle, stab the wispy bits of the leg into the body so that the leg is loosely attached.

7

Next, place one of the other legs towards the wispy end of the body using the technique in step 6 to attach it. Make sure that the feet on the legs are both facing towards the wispy end of the body. Turn the body over and attach the two remaining legs in the same way, positioning the feet in the same direction.

8

To add shape and strength to the body, turn the body upside down on the foam block and place a large wisp of cream wool on the belly. Stab the wool in with the single needle, allowing the outer wisps to adhere along the inside of the legs and down the sides of the body. Add more wisps of cream wool to the underside, stabbing it in and working towards the back and front of the body

Wisps are your friend in this project, helping you to achieve a smooth, soft finish.

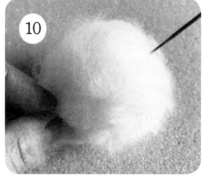

Try to get the basic structure of the polar bear firm before adding the features.

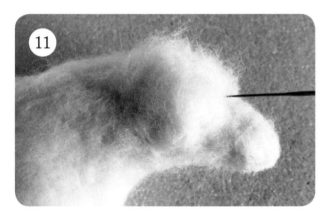

9

Turn the polar bear's body onto its side. Take some more cream wool and, using both hands, pull it into a loop. Place the loop directly onto the body at the top of one of the attached legs. Using the single needle, stab in the loop, working the wispy parts down the leg. Repeat this on all the legs to make them stronger.

10

To make the head, take a small amount of cream wool and use both hands to pull it into a balloon shape. Lay the balloon shape on the foam block. While holding the wispy ends in one hand, stab all over with the single needle, rotating the piece until it has shrunk in size slightly and is denser to the touch. Position the ball on the wispy end of the body, stabbing in the wisps from both sections so they attach to each other. Stab in some cream wool around the join to start forming the polar bear's neck.

11

For the muzzle, make a small ball using the same technique as in step 10 and attach it in the same way to the front of the head. Add wisps of cream wool around the join to start forming the muzzle. Use the single needle to sculpt the face by stabbing indentations either side of the muzzle and adding wisps of cream wool to pad out the cheek area.

12

Now make the first ear. Take a small amount of cream wool, pull it into a loop, then place it on the foam block. While holding the wispy ends with one hand, stab the loop with the single needle to form a small round shape, working your way out from the centre. Lift the ear off the foam, turn it over and continue to stab with the needle. Add a small amount of dark grey wool to the centre of the ear, stabbing lightly so it doesn't come through to the back. Repeat this process to make the second ear.

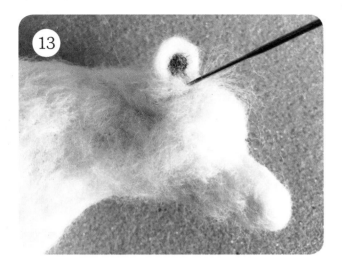

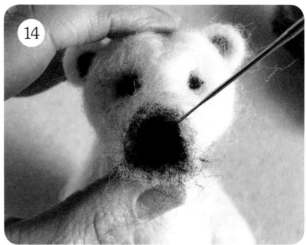

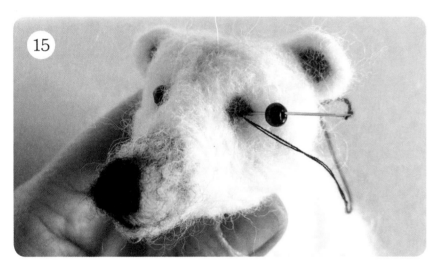

13

Attach the ears by placing them to the side of the head and stabbing in the wispy ends with the single needle. Add small wisps of cream wool to the front of the ears and in between to blend and shape the top part of the polar bear's forehead. Next take a thin wisp of dark grey wool and place it on the end of the muzzle. Stab it in with the needle, blending it in with wisps of cream wool.

14

To start on the eyes, stab a wisp of dark grey wool into the indentations made in step 11. Then place a wisp of black wool right at the tip of the muzzle, stabbing a few times in the same spot to attach it. Stab in the remaining wisps of black wool to form the nose. Under the nose, place a small wisp of black wool, stab it once, then pull it down to one side to create a small line for the mouth. Stab the needle along the line to secure and repeat this process for the other side.

15

To finish the eyes, take the sewing needle and black thread, knot one end and sew on the black beads for the eyes in the indentations. Knot the thread around the last bead and fasten off through the back of the polar bear's head.

16

Finally, stab in large wisps of cream wool to the top, rear and tummy of the polar bear, adding more to the areas where needed. This will give some density to the bear, filling it out and smoothing the surface. For the tail, take a wisp of cream wool, form a small triangular shape and place it on the foam block. Stab with the single needle, lifting and turning it over and stabbing until it has shrunk and become denser. Place the tail on to the rear of the polar bear and stab it in to attach, adding fine wisps of cream wool to smooth over any joins.

Suppliers

For wool, felting needles, needle holders and leather finger protectors

UK

The Felt Box Ltd
73 Oak Lane
Kings Cliffe
Peterborough
PE8 6YY
thefeltbox.co.uk

World of Wool
Unit 8, The Old Railway Goods Yard
Scar Lane
Huddersfield
West Yorkshire
HD3 4PE
worldofwool.co.uk

USA

Living Felt
2440 E HWY 290
Ste E1
Dripping Springs
TX 78620
livingfelt.com

For upholstery foam blocks

UK

Fiveways Floors
fivewaysfloors.co.uk

The Foam Shop
thefoamshop.co.uk

USA

Joann
joann.com

For general art and craft supplies

UK

Fabricland
fabricland.co.uk

Hobbycraft
hobbycraft.co.uk

USA

Michaels
www.michaels.com

For jute string

UK

Hobbycraft
hobbycraft.co.uk

Millbrook Garden Centres
millbrookgc.co.uk

Nutscene
nutscene.com

USA

Michaels
www.michaels.com

Index

Acknowledgements

This book was only possible with the help and support of my wonderful family: Joe, my husband and best friend; Will and Lucia, the most understanding children a mother could ever wish for, and my fantastic brothers and sisters, Louise, Daniel, Richard, Victoria and Alex. I would also like to say thank you to my friends who believed in me, and everyone at GMC Publications who was a part of this book. Finally, I have dedicated this book to the two most important people who supported me my whole life, and who made me who I am today: my dear mum and dad, who are sadly no longer with us.

Thank you all.

First published 2019 by Guild of Master Craftsman Publications Ltd, Castle Place, 166 High Street, Lewes, East Sussex BN7 1XU, UK

Reprinted 2021

Text © Emma Herian, 2019

Copyright in the Work © GMC Publications Ltd, 2019

ISBN 978 1 78494 515 2

Publisher: Jonathan Bailey
Production Manager: Jim Bulley
Senior Project Editor: Wendy McAngus
Editor: Nicola Hodgson
Managing Art Editor: Gilda Pacitti
Art Editor: Rebecca Mothersole
Photographers: Rebecca Mothersole and Andrew Perris
Step photographer: Emma Herian

Colour origination by GMC Reprographics

Printed in China

To place an order, contact:
GMC Publications Ltd
Castle Place,
166 High Street, Lewes,
East Sussex, BN7 1XU
United Kingdom
Tel: +44 (0)1273 488005